MW01626365

WHEN THE PORCH LIGHT'S ON...

Stories of People, Popcorn and Parasails

Library of Congress Cataloging-in-Publication

ISBN 1-879234-56-4

Second Edition

10 9 8 7 6 5 4 3 2 1

Published by
Cross Roads Press
Fort Worth, Texas

Printed in the United States

Dedication

This book is dedicated
To the women in my life
Who have always outvoted me, 4-1.
Their love and support are beyond measure—
My wife of 36 years, Brenda Carol
And our three wonderful daughters—
Julie (Mrs. Bryan) Choate
Jana (Mrs. Kyle) Penney
and
Jeanie (Mrs. Ryan) McDaniel

Acknowledgements

One of life's greatest discoveries is that each of us has mentors—from the first moments when we have at least a fuzzy knowledge of what "no" means until those last days, when we are looking for a "yes"—even if by lip-reading—much of the time. They are everywhere, these mentors, long after formal education has ended. They are treasures, worthy of reverence and acknowledgement.

They are family, friends and associates—people from whom I have had opportunity to learn life's greatest lessons. They've been the seasoning in the soup of life, providing excitement, acceptance, love and good humor.

How thankful I am to have had the chance to see life from many sides. With training in journalism and experience both in the print and electronic media, I have learned what deadlines mean and the importance of truth. Then, for almost two decades, I was on the other side of the microphone and desktop—involved more in answering than in asking.

Bill Moyers, press secretary to President Lyndon B. Johnson, espoused an intriguing credo for his role, which called for him "to tell the truth whenever possible, but never lie." That's not a bad goal, is it? So, I salute my mentors, many of whom know who they are, and some who never will. A dream is that all the people I love will be able to identify such friends and encouragers all along the way.

I have arrived at that place where additional words seem futile—just as they did late in my 40th and final year of work in higher education. A Howard Payne University freshman, dead serious, stopped me on campus one day to ask "if I'd ever seen a real typewriter up close." My eye twitched a bit as I started groping for an answer before he added, "I don't think I'd even know how to plug one in." At once I knew that a detailed answer would be pointless. "Why yes, I have…." And I shut up. And walked away….

But, seriously folks, there are two people I want to acknowledge by name. One is a man who entrusted Howard Payne University to further the education of his son, Josh—a nationally-honored student athlete (two words that don't always go together). This proud dad has been a constant encourager. He is a fellow journalist and the author of countless books. I refer to Caleb Pirtle, who has been an invaluable advisor in this literary effort. But I decided to ignore his advice, and write the book anyway….

And it wouldn't be finished yet if Julie, our oldest daughter, hadn't shown up in the final days, handed Ben off to his grandmother, pushed me aside and commandeered the keyboard for final corrections and editing….

About the Author

Dr. Don Newbury was born on September 7, 1937 to Mr. and Mrs. T. J. Newbury.

He was educated in Early Public Schools, near Brownwood, Texas and is a 1956 graduate. Growing up in the shadows of Howard Payne University, he enrolled there that fall, completing his baccalaureate degree five years later with majors in journalism, business and secondary education. Subsequent diplomas were from the University of Texas in 1966 (Master of Journalism degree) and the University of North Texas in 1973 (Ph.D. degree in Higher Education Administration). Post-doctoral study in university public relations was at the University of Notre Dame.

Dr. Newbury's final 15 years in higher education administration were spent at his alma mater in Brownwood. He was the first HPU graduate holding a baccalaureate degree from the 112-year-old school to return as its President. He served in that role from 1985 until 1997, when he was named Chancellor. He retired there in August of 2000, and the Board of Trustees asked him to retain the title of Chancellor.

Earlier, he had served as Instructor of Journalism at Howard Payne (1960-63); Director of College Information and Instructor of Journalism at Sul Ross State University, Alpine, Texas (1963-67); Director of Community Relations at Tarrant County Junior College, Fort Worth,

Texas (1967-80), and President of Western Texas College, Snyder, Texas (1980-85).

An honorary life member of the National Congress of Parents and Teachers (PTA) and Phi Theta Kappa, national community/junior college honors organization, Dr. Newbury has held numerous organizational positions during his career, including presidencies of the Association of Texas Junior Colleges, Association of Church-Related Universities of the South, Association of Southern Baptist Colleges and Schools and the American Southwest Athletic Conference.

He has been cited as "alumnus of the year" by HPU, and when the School of Education at the University of North Texas elected to honor an educator annually, he was the initial recipient of the Dr. J. C. Matthews Award. (Dr. Matthews was a long-time UNT President who taught there several years following his retirement from the presidency. Dr. Newbury was privileged to be in his classes.)

He and his wife, the former Brenda Pack, have been married for 36 years. She was a high school teacher for a few years prior to the birth of their first daughter, Julie. Life then centered on being a mother, and with subsequent arrivals of Jana and Jeanie, she had plenty to do.

◆ ◆ ◆

Contents

INTRODUCTION

Previews of Coming Infractions

AN OFT-HEARD line reads, "Keep your mouth shut and let people think you are an idiot. Open your mouth and remove all doubt!"

Those words seem ever so applicable to me as I wade out into deep autobiographical waters, attempting to be fair in presenting facts as I remember them, even if I miss some of them by a zip code or two! In a few places, my reflections fall into the "may have happened" category....

When one looks back on a 40-year career in higher education, much has to be re-claimed strictly from memory—mine or others. As chapters are stacked upon chapters, thought turns to what the book might be entitled. Dozens of possibilities were wadded up and tossed, the way they do in the movies. In the final days of writing, I felt the pressure to come up with a title, and thankfully, a daughter came through! Our youngest, Jeanie McDaniel, who has always shared her dad's delight in a good story or a good football or basketball game on television, suggested the title chosen: *When the Porch Light's On...Stories of People, Popcorn and Parasails.*

◆ ◆ ◆

I acknowledge her contribution, as well as her proofreading and editing assistance. Similar credit goes to her sisters, Jana Penney and Julie Choate, and to their mother, Brenda Newbury, who has been right beside me for more than 95% of the education years and all of the presidential ones. (Family friend Michelle Clark provided much assistance.)

Instructed that titles these days usually run pretty long, I figured the one Jeanie suggested qualifies. Preachers sometimes mention their "Mother Hubbard sermons," which, like Mother Hubbard dresses, cover everything but touch nothing! That description pretty much fits my literary effort!

Please allow me to dissect the title. "When the porch light's on" highlights a period of almost 15 years during which a balcony light turned on at 701 Center Avenue in Brownwood (the Howard Payne University president's home) meant hot popcorn was being served on the back porch. This period represents about half the time I have given away popcorn. The most magical time was in Brownwood, where many conversations, challenges and joys were discussed with bags of popcorn in hand. We popped about a ton of corn annually for HPU students, employees, campus visitors and to share at speaking engagements. For the latter, we used large cellophane bags, printed with the words "Presidential Popcorn—Howard Payne University, Brownwood, Texas." So now you know, if you didn't already, that this book is a collection of stories, many of which are about the "popcorn president."

◆ ◆ ◆

But, it's more than that. Experiences, remarks and foibles noted along the way—drawn from my life and those of others—are re-visited. During my undergraduate years, Mr. Ralph Marshall, then bookstore manager, golf coach and bowling teacher (folks had to hold down multiple jobs then, too) maintained that if a person has just three real friends in life—over its course—he is fortunate indeed. At the time, I disagreed; now, in retrospect, I realize that for many people, this is probably fairly accurate. How blessed I count myself to have many friends—friends who have encouraged, assisted and been "caught up" in the critical importance of education—every step of the way.

So we've covered the porch light, people and popcorn. Now, what about the parasail? About a half-dozen years into the presidency at HPU, Lynn Nabers, a member of the Board of Trustees, asked what I did for leisure. I responded that I liked to make speeches and pop corn. "You need a boat to really relax," he suggested, perhaps largely because he had a boat to sell....Indeed, the 18-foot sports boat, powered by a 200HP engine, was only a few years old. His sons were away at college, so it was now largely idle, and a good buy at just $4,500.

Owning a boat had never really occurred to me. I don't think Brenda and I had been on the water more than two or three times in the previous 30 years. A few years earlier, the girls had mentioned wanting one, and I told them to go with their friends who had boats, and they did. Acquiring one was a difficult decision. But, the seller was a board member eager to sell his boat; it became easier to decide. It was a fine boat, and maybe it would be fun. Finally, as I pointed out to Brenda, "We're not buying a ranch!" We bought the boat and I took it out a few times; I was bored stiff.

◆ ◆ ◆

One day, I pulled the boat trailer through the campus, inviting students to accompany me to the lake. From that day forward, there were usually 8-10 takers (or more), and away we went, slowly building the inventory to include skiis, wakeboards, slaloms, kneeboards and such. We had a ton of fun, and the kids were happy to clean and polish the boat every time upon return to the campus.

A few years later I watched parasailing on television and was immediately intrigued by the sport. I was able to buy a used sail and rig up a towing apparatus behind the boat. Thankfully, an HPU alumnus owned an "open spot" on the west shore of the main body of Lake Brownwood. He gave permission for us to use his shoreline for parasail lift-offs. (Usually, this worked fine—if the wind was no faster than 15 MPH and blowing from the southeast. Generally, this seemed a prevailing condition.) A few times, there were crosswinds, or crossed-up instructions, and flyers were scratched a bit by tree limbs. Undaunted, the sport was pursued, signal flags obtained and minor adjustments made. More students wanted to fly than time and conditions would permit. If we were able to fly two in an hour, that wasn't a bad deal at all.

After providing 10 minutes of flying, we would slow the boat, allowing the parasailor to float to splashdown. Then, we'd pick up the flyer and sail, go back to shore, untangle the lines and go again. (Flyers would get into the harness, then stand, as long as they physically could, some 40 feet from the water. When the sail filled with air, helpers hoisted the white flag, signaling me to take off at top speed. Flyers then ran toward the lake, hoping to be airborne by the time they reached the water. Usually, it worked....)

◆ ◆ ◆

As news of the parasailing spread about, demand grew. Then, during a trip to Gulf Shores, Alabama, to visit a benefactress and valued friend, Dr. Grace Pilot, I took note of a sign at the Alabama Parasailing dock: "Parasail Boat for Sale." It was no doubt a sign from heaven! From this point on, the parasailing experience became much more predictable and professional.

Upon return to Brownwood, I contacted several friends of the university. We pooled our resources to come up with the $30,000 needed for the boat and supplies and moved it to Lake Brownwood. During two summers there, more than 600 youngsters parasailed, including numerous church youth groups from around the state. It was a fine recruiting tool since it gave prospects the chance to get to know some real life HPU students. It also was exhilarating to be around such elation! All the kids (whether junior high or high school students) tried hard to be "macho" about the upcoming lift into the sky. In truth, most were frightened about the unknown, but just about always had a "piece of cake" attitude about it when they landed on the platform, a 10'x10' area on the back of the 32-foot boat.

When they landed, the parasail remained filled with air, and the boat was maneuvered slowly forward until the next flyer was secured, and then, it was full speed ahead. (A bar, capable of carrying weight up to 400 pounds, allowed as many as three lightweights to fly at once....For junior high girls, three was a favorite number....)

◆ ◆ ◆

Oh my goodness! There are so many parasailing memories. A junior high school youth group from Lubbock seemed to hang on every word as I explained safety features involved in parasailing. "Be sure to take off your caps," I warned. In an instant, the kids removed their caps, and in some cases, caps were placed over their hearts. "No, I didn't mean take your caps off now," I explained. "But if you don't when you fly, they'll blow away...." One youngster, not fully understanding that the harness was held by strong ropes to the parasail, asked, "What if we get tired and turn loose?" As they flew, a CD player belted out strong "flying music," including "A New Way to Fly" and "I'll Fly Away."

Dr. Thurston Dean, an orthopedic surgeon in Midland who served for several years on the HPU Board of Trustees, responded this way about parasail safety: "When proper safety precautions are observed, I think parasailing is safer than many other lake sports," he said. "I have never treated a parasail injury, never known any physician who has and have never read of a parasailor being treated medically....Of course, if you have a REALLY BIG accident, the ambulance might as well just bypass the hospital!"

◆ ◆ ◆

Thankfully, there were no REALLY BIG accidents in our lake adventures—except one. It didn't involve the parasail, but I was the victim! (It is arguable whether it was REALLY BIG, but this description, like surgery, depends on whether it's yours or someone else's.) One evening, near sundown, most students had gone back to campus, but Dan Murray (now Captain/Dr. Dan Murray, a flight surgeon in the Air Force), begged for just one more ride on the wakeboard. When he finally cratered following a lengthy ride, he yelled for help, screaming that his foot was broken, and he couldn't get it out of the wakeboard binding....

I pulled the boat along side, killed the engine and jumped in, realizing that I needed to get him into the boat, and perhaps to the hospital. I swam toward him, grabbed his arm and started pulling him toward the boat. My left pinky finger came in contact with the idle boat prop, and I sustained a deep cut. Blood spurted, and at the same moment, Dan pulled his foot free, minimizing his injury, saying, "I'm going to be fine." "I'm not; get me to the hospital," I responded, blood pouring from my finger. Several stitches were required to close the wound, and now I cannot play the piano. (But, I have to admit, I couldn't play the piano before the accident, either....)

◆ ◆ ◆

"Dunking" is a favorite part of parasailing, and this involves dropping the flyer into the water about waist-deep, then taking off again. When I went to pick up the boat in Alabama, the folks there gave me a ride on a 1200-foot rope. Dan and another student, Zeb Alexander, went along to learn how to be deck hands. I saw them gesturing as I began my descent. You guessed it—they ordered me dunked!

So, that's the story of the title. I've been introduced at speakers' podiums a good many times as "the nation's 'unstuffiest' college president." I hope you feel this introduction is appropriate. It is likewise important that you believe I do recognize "serious as serious and fun as fun." I know the difference, and can deal with both! I hope you enjoy this book as much as I have enjoyed the experiences along the way. That's a lofty expectation....

Don Newbury
Fort Worth, Texas
August 1, 2002

Chapter One

When I Was 'This Tall'

It is hard to imagine any person, anywhere or any time, being so blessed by family, and these blessings have continued throughout my life. My parents were the late Mr. and Mrs. T. J. Newbury. Both were from big families, both had little formal education (neither finished high school), and both were familiar and comfortable with hard work. My mom's mother died during the national flu epidemic around 1930, and Mom—the oldest of three girls among nine children—helped her dad raise the younger siblings. My dad, born in Louisiana to a railroad family, had seven brothers and sisters, one of whom was claimed by diphtheria at an early age. Mom (the former Tempie Gotcher) and Dad (Thomas J. Newbury) met when both families lived in rural Brown County, when the country was in the depths of the Great Depression. When they married in 1931, they scratched out a living in farm work, including long days picking cotton bolls, sometimes moving around West Texas to the next fields needing cotton pickers.

I was born September 7, 1937, in their small rented farmhouse west of May, Texas. Dr. McDaniel drove out to the farm for the delivery, and Dad joked many times about how the doctor charged him $25—and that I probably wasn't worth it! In those days, it was common to be born at home. (I was not to be hospitalized—not even once—until open-heart surgery required it 60 years later.) Soon after my birth, my dad got a job with May Schools. He was custodian, "fix-it" man, bus driver and you name it—there were no written job descriptions. He eagerly did whatever "Mr. White" (H. E. White, Superintendent of Schools) asked him to do. After all, the school paid him $30 a month....

I'm not sure how we got around—most likely, we didn't go many places. When we did, I think we either walked or hitched rides with friends fortunate enough to own motorized transportation and generous enough to share it. I do recall riding the school bus routes with my dad; I was about three years of age. I remember his cheery countenance as he drove the lumbering yellow bus over the country roads, and how he encouraged all the riders....He was mighty proud to be a part of May Schools, even though his "position" was several cuts below a professional one, and I doubt very much if he had ever heard the word "contract." If he had, he would have consulted Superintendent White to make sure he should sign it. Dad was usually leery about signing his name on anything, and he urged me repeatedly to be careful what I put my name on....

One of my earliest memories concerns Friday night movies at the school. I was fascinated by the guy who knew how to thread the projector, and how quickly he could take off one reel of the old black and white film and slip on the next one with minimal delay. The projector was noisy, the picture sometimes jumped and the film almost always broke at least once. They took up a collection to rent another film for the next week, and there was free popcorn, lemonade and "Polly-Pop" for us kids. ("Polly-Pop" was a precursor of Kool-Aid.) Life was exceedingly uncomplicated....

◆ ◆ ◆

In 1940, our lives changed greatly. Mr. White changed professions, becoming principal owner of the Central Texas Gas Company, a small firm providing natural gas for several rural communities in Brown County. Dad was loyal to Mr. White, taking a similar multi-task job with the new company. Our family moved a dozen miles east to Blanket. I doubt that our economic status improved much, but the company provided free housing, a pick-up truck that we could also use as a personal vehicle, and a telephone! The phone, of course, was critical to my dad's work. He had to be accessible in case of emergencies. There were few phones in the community, and many neighbors borrowed ours. A ring of "one long and two shorts" caused our phone to clang, and others up and down the party line could listen if they chose.

Part of my dad's job included making monthly rounds to pick up payments for gas at several grocery stores in the county where customers left payments. They had no meters for gas usage; they simply paid $2 in summer months and $4 in the winter. I marveled at people paying so much for this utility every single month!

At age five, I moved to the country again (as if the early years in May and Blanket were urban). The family moved to the Salt Creek Community, about eight miles west of Blanket and a dozen miles from Brownwood, county seat of Brown County. The house redefined modesty. It had a kitchen, bedroom and living room. My bed was in the living room. There was a bathroom with a commode and lavatory, but a washtub was brought in for bathing. A few years later, Dad hired a man to pour concrete for a makeshift shower, and Dad walled it with planks on three sides. Had there been a door, it would have looked exactly like an "out" house "in" doors....

This Old House...
Our Salt Creek home, where we moved when I was 5, living there until age 15. Long abandoned in this picture, it was little better at its best—except glass was usually in the windows.

The move to Salt Creek put Dad closer to several gas wells that supplied the company, and there was plenty of room to store steel pipe used in the natural gas lines. Though I lived in the country, I was anything but a "country boy." I don't think I ever milked a cow and gathered but few eggs. Costs of allergic reactions to cotton fields put an end to that, and working with barnyard animals never piqued my interest. I rode a school bus to Early School, where I attended all 12 grades. This was about a 10-mile ride each way, with arrival back home each afternoon leaving time to ride my bike, skip rocks on a farm pond or fire my air rifle. (Often, I emptied entire packages of BB's into the armor of armadillos, never fazing them....)

◆ ◆ ◆

It is not possible to think about that air rifle without remembering a bleak moment, perhaps when I was 10 years of age or so, when I wondered if a BB would penetrate the glass on the gasoline pump we had on the place. It was a primitive pump—Dad would move the handle, forward and back, to force about ten gallons of gasoline into the glass cylinder. I was fascinated to see gas slosh about, then disappear when Dad put the nozzle into the truck's gasoline tank. I had sense enough to know that I would NEVER pull the trigger of my air rifle anywhere even close to the pump, fearful of the possible dangerous result of mixing BB's and gasoline....Still, I wondered many times if a BB would penetrate that gasoline cylinder.

One day, with Dad away and the cylinder empty, my boyish curiosity begged to be satisfied. I drew a bead on the upper part of the cylinder, and pulled the trigger. I was mortified to see a tiny hole appear in the glass; I had figured the BB would simply glance off the surface.

I was hopeful that my dad might not notice the hole right away, but he was bound to see gasoline when it came spurting out....

Before the inevitable spanking was administered, I tried to reason with him that if he would pump eight gallons into the cylinder instead of ten, the gasoline level would never reach the hole. He didn't like my logic, but had to follow it for years. He made me realize there was a price to be paid for unhealthy curiosity.

◆ ◆ ◆

WHEN MY BROTHER, Fred, was born, I was seven years of age. We seemed to be from two generations. Immediately, I felt almost old enough to be a babysitter. In the early years, we had little in common except the affection we both felt for our mongrel dog, Prince.

A favorite summertime activity was forcing bunny rabbits out of the six-inch pipes stacked on racks near our house. It was a simple procedure. I placed a coffee can inside the pipe, using a metal rod to push the can 30 or 40 feet through the pipe. At the other end, I stationed Fred and Prince. Sometimes we would catch the bunnies in gunny sacks; other times we both delighted in just watching Prince take off after them....

A seemingly failsafe way to determine if rabbits were seeking a shaded respite in the pipes from the hot summer sun was simply to peer inside. If the view was obscured, or if we saw two bunny ears erect, it was almost certain that a rabbit was blocking the view. One day, we were wrong, very wrong....

Seeing what I thought was a rabbit, I pushed the coffee can through the pipe, with Fred and Prince "at the ready," gunny sack in place for the catch. When our prey hit the sack, Fred held it tight, and Prince pawed at the bag like crazy. In an instant, both brother and dog looked sick. I wanted to go help them, but the odor was too great. Our "rabbit" that day was a petrified skunk, but this little creature was not so petrified that he could not make both Fred and Prince smell like a skunk's siblings for the next several days....

◆ ◆ ◆

Entertainment was mostly "42" (a game played with dominoes) with relatives and friends, and in those days, there were "drop-in" visits. It was not uncommon for relatives to land on us (or us on them) completely unannounced, and almost always at mealtime. This was the "expected" thing, and Mom always hustled about to make sure there was plenty of food. After supper, kids played croquet, pitched washers and horseshoes, or shot baskets while the domino games kept the adults busy, often well into the night. While they played, amidst the plethora of boasts, bluffs and threats, they caught up on the news of the day. Upon becoming totally "tuckered out," the kids curled up on pallets when their bodies insisted that rest could no longer be ignored....

About once a week, Mom and Dad would take me to the movies in Brownwood. This modest entertainment was not as "tame" as it would seem. Remember, there was no television in those days. When World War II broke out, the army's Camp Bowie, located a couple of miles from Brownwood, became a military center, doubling the county's population in a short period of time. Most of the soldiers lived in tents, but when they had a pass, or even a few hours off, they "went to the picture show." (That's what we called movies back then.) Though they had theatres on base, current releases played in the downtown theatres.

World War II Uniform? Well, sort of. I called it my "army suit," and this photo was made soon after my fifth birthday. It was about the time that Brownwood teemed with the military personnel of Camp Bowie. I was horrified at the thought of getting lost in the masses on the crowded streets. Brownwood had eight downtown movie theatres at the time.

A typical procedure involved ticket purchasing, then munching on a bag of popcorn, waiting until the feature ended. When it did, soldiers poured out of the theatre, and those of us outside poured in, trying to enter early enough to get seats that weren't too close to the screen. (Seated way down front, we had to look up at the screen, often getting cricks in our necks.)

I remember holding on to my folks' hands for dear life, because soldiers were everywhere. I knew there was no reason to be afraid of them, but, at age five or so, I had a horror of getting lost in the big crowded city! Youngsters today can't believe that in those days there were eight theatres in downtown Brownwood, and in the 1950's, three drive-in theatres. (There now are only about a dozen drive-in theatres in the entire state!) Theatre admission was 35 cents and 12 cents for children under age 12 at the best "picture show," the Bowie Theatre. At most of the others, it scaled downward to 25 cents and 9 cents.

I THINK I was "under 12" until I was well into my 13th year, perfecting, as did my friends, the rehearsed art of "slouching down" in front of the cashier's booth, meekly asking for a child's admission. The savvy cashier no doubt knew of the ploy, but also knew that whatever money we had left would be spent just a few feet away at the concession stand. (One Saturday, the carnival came to town, and I had to be "short" and "tall" on the same day! I was "short" when admitted to the movie, but stood on tip-toe at the sign where they made sure you were tall enough to ride on the carnival's bumper cars. You had to reach a minimal height of "this tall," or they wouldn't sell you a ticket....)

One time, we had more fun AFTER the carnival left town. We kids biked to the deserted carnival grounds, going over the area sort of like guys with metal detectors might do, except we had no such equipment. Our search was limited to what we could see. What we saw was the "you must be this tall" sign; perhaps it had fallen off the truck. We took it home, and thought of some creative re-wording. Turning it sideways, we painted the words: WEENIE DOG CONTEST SATURDAY—entries must be THIS LONG. We leaned it up against the vet's front door that night, then ran away pronto. It was the laugh of the town the next day....

◆ ◆ ◆

All of my family loved Early Schools, where Fred and I completed public school—me in 1956; him in 1963. We didn't miss many school activities. I excelled in several "county meet" literary events (now called University Interscholastic League), and Fred was several cuts above average in both football and basketball. Sadly, I didn't see many of his games because I was deeply involved in sports information work for Howard Payne University, as well as covering numerous games for the BROWNWOOD BULLETIN and Radio Station KBWD.

Fred and I were loved, encouraged and disciplined. Both of our parents regretted not having more formal education, and they spoke often of "when the boys go to college." It was never IF, but WHEN....In fact, Dad often said, "Don, we'll help you get through Howard Payne, and then maybe you can help Fred."

That's exactly what happened. I earned enough money to pay all direct college expenses, but I was allowed to live at home, and was provided food and clothing. (When Fred entered first grade, Mom started working in sales/alterations at Brownwood department stores, earning little more than minimum wage.) In 1955, they borrowed

$2,800 to build a four-room frame home in Early. This time, my brother and I had a bedroom to share. (More than once I've wondered how they handled this debt so quickly. It was a 3% note and was paid off in three years.) In the mid-1950's, Central Texas Gas Company was sold to Lone Star Gas Company, and Dad worked there until retirement around 1970. He never earned as much as $600 per month....

Howard Payne Staffer

This photograph was made around 1960. Notice state-of-the-art IBM Selectric typewriter (salesman assured me it was the only one in Brown County at the time and certainly the only one at Howard Payne). I bought it myself. Notice neat shelves, desk, filing trays, etc.

Finishing HPU in 1961 with a triple major, I stayed on to teach journalism and help with college information duties for a couple of years. Then, in 1963, I left home for the first time; it was the best move of my life. I was 25 years of age, and accepted the "lofty" position of "Director of College Information and Instructor of Journalism" at Sul

Ross State University in Alpine. It was a queasy feeling, not only leaving home for the first time, but moving 330 miles away. SRSU's offer of $5,400 a year, plus a free room in the men's honors dorm if I would direct it, seemed like a ton of money. (I had earned $3,000 and $3,600, respectively, during my first two years out of college at HPU; when Dr. Guy D. Newman, my president, learned of my offer at Sul Ross, he offered to equal it.)

Though much of my heart was at HPU, I couldn't bear to accept such a big salary from a small, church-supported school where the never-ending struggle to meet monthly payrolls was a way of life for several generations....Dr. Newman remained a close friend and loyal supporter throughout his life, championing me every step of the way.

◆ ◆ ◆

Chapter Two

Of Chickens, Rabbits, and Such

The word "chicken" elicits smiles, if not outright chuckles. Mere thoughts of this bird, gangly and way down on the IQ chain, conjure up a multitude of images and funny stories....

Dr. Reagan Brown, former Texas Commissioner of Agriculture, entertained around the state with such stories many thousands of times. He sounded more rural than he actually was, but audiences, "citified" or not, loved his stories. Particularly popular was his account of growing-up days when he claimed to be a "chicken-turner" on the family farm. Listeners did some head turning, shifting gazes toward others to see if fellow listeners had an inkling of what a chicken-turner might do. Usually, at least for a few minutes, audiences were clueless, unless they had heard him speak previously....

Soon, though, they exploded in laughter when he explained what chicken-turners do. Dr. Brown explained that on the farm, chickens would "roost" each evening around the rim of their cistern, the source of the family's cool, clear drinking water. In fact, to get a dipper of water after sundown, one had to push chickens aside....Brown said that the chickens' usual roosting formation was

apprehension about being the only guy in the class with only a barnyard cat and a mongrel dog between me and total "animallessness," despite our living out in the country. (Cats and dogs, by the way, don't qualify for 4-H projects.) He said students with limited livestock opportunities sometimes chose rabbits, with a buck and a doe often producing multiple litters of bunnies during a school year. Eureka! I could join the ranks of animal owners; my livestock background was a lot worse than limited.

I digress. My original intention was to get right into an "I'm-not-making-this-up" story about "rabbit-turning," thus linking it with Brown's yarn about "chicken-turning." Allow me to fast-forward to springtime of my freshman year. It was "County Meet Time" (translation: livestock competition in Brown County). I was hanging around the rabbit area with zero chance of getting a ribbon. Alas, I had no entry, but I could at least associate with those who did....

Remember, rabbits were no higher than third-tier as animal project choices among students in my class. Only a few kids—usually living in town and limited to backyards for livestock projects—chose rabbits, and even fewer raised chickens. I had plenty of room, but, for reasons cited earlier, I bought a pair of rabbits as animals of choice....

◆ ◆ ◆

Again, digression, and apologies are in order. It won't happen again, probably. As mentioned, it was county meet time, and youngsters from all over the county brought their entries, groomed for judging. Most of the crowds, of course, gathered around the cattle, horses, sheep and hogs. They even had a "paid judge," a bright young man with two college degrees and only a whisker away from a doctorate.

That judge was Dick Eudaly, now a good friend at Travis Avenue Baptist Church in Fort Worth; he had studied at three of the foremost "ag" universities in the world—Oklahoma State, Texas Tech and Texas A&M. In total awe, we applauded him generously. He smiled at us, acting as if he were more than competent to judge any sort of animal competition. Stifling a yawn, he gave the impression that judging animals at our county meet would be a breeze. (Usually, such judges gave ribbons for cattle, hogs, sheep and goats, and a lesser judge, almost always a volunteer, ranked the rabbits, because at many shows, there were no rabbits.)

The young man wasn't visibly shaken (remember, he already had two degrees) when the contest chairman revealed a definite problem—the guy who had agreed to judge rabbits didn't show, and there were several to be judged. The young Cowboy/Red Raider/Aggie was asked (actually, it was more of a plea) if he would judge the rabbit competition as well. Swelling with confidence, he responded, "Of course I will." (Keep in mind that he had never judged rabbits or even seen it done....)

"Are they fryers or breeding rabbits?" the young man asked, his response implying that he knew something about one or the other. The director answered, "Fryers," and the response seemed to relieve the deputized judge greatly. He gave the impression that he could judge fryers with an eye closed. Breeding rabbits? Not so sure. (Decades later, he admitted that whichever competition awaited—fryers or breeders—THAT would have been his area of expertise.)

Dick later confessed that all he knew about rabbits was that they had floppy ears, pink eyes and twitchy noses—essentially the same facts known by pre-schoolers whose parents read to them at bedtime....(This admission came, however, many years later when rabbit ribbons were faded. We "formerly unsteady freshmen" are now unsteady in other ways. Many have grandchildren showing animals in competition, and—surprise, surprise—are studying in "co-ed" agriculture and home economics classes! From what I understand, not many students choose rabbits for show animals today, either....)

BACK TO THE contest. The judge went straight to the rabbit tent, where a bunch of wide-eyed freshmen had their entries lined up, steadying them with their hands around the rabbits' rumps that rested on rickety pedestals. He walked up and down, carefully eyeing each entry, much the way he would look at calves. Calves, though, were led around the ring, so they could be viewed from every angle. Dare he ask the kids to lead their rabbits around the ring? He thought not.

Realizing that "fryers" meant that the rabbits were raised for frying pans, the judge figured most of the meat would be found in the rear areas. He couldn't see those parts; that's where the youngsters were holding them down. Then, he had an idea! "Reverse the rabbits!" he ordered. (Dick swore later he had never heard the Reagan Brown chicken-turner story. He said this was the only way he knew to examine the "meaty" parts.)

The kids stared at each other in disbelief! They had practiced showing their rabbits, but had never heard such a request. They would have been no more surprised if the judge had ordered them to drop their pants! (High school freshmen, in those days, did exactly what teachers asked. If he had told them to start their engines, they would have looked for engines to start.) Tediously and slowly, they turned their animals' "rumps outward," trying, as best they could, to steady their bunnies by holding on to their front legs. The rabbits fidgeted, not accustomed to being in such poses. (I laughed at the "what if" thought of having an entry. Mine would likely have wound up sideways! My buck and doe, as you'll soon see, had nothing to show for their efforts.)

Sensing their discomfort, the judge realized that with just a few word strokes, he had painted himself into the smallest of corners. What to do? He did what seemed most logical, given the rabbits' new positions. He methodically felt the rump of each rabbit, humming softly as he made pencil notes. He determined which rabbits were "rumpiest" and awarded ribbons accordingly. No eyebrows were raised, not even one. The kids just figured this was a new rabbit-judging technique, introduced and perfected at one of those great universities—perhaps researched at all three—and was just now making its way to our part of the country....

◆ ◆ ◆

Now, I return to my sad agricultural efforts. Though "rabbit-turning," like "chicken-turning," is funny at the very thought, my efforts to raise rabbits in the high school 4–H club weren't funny and weren't successful. As my teacher suggested, I bought a full-grown buck and doe and built my own rabbit hutch, using apple boxes and some used chicken wire. I whistled while I worked, thinking in single dimension: keeping the rabbits INSIDE the hutch. I gave no thought to hutch predators from the OUTSIDE. I use the word "hutch" as often as I can, because every time I said "cage" around Mr. Wheeler, he corrected me. (Critical error number one: Use half-inch hail screen, not two-inch chicken wire, for the hutch. No one was that specific about how to build the hutch.)

Sure enough, in a few weeks, I was more than excited to find eight wiggly bunnies when I went to feed one morning. I couldn't wait to tell the teacher of my good fortune. Dollar signs filled my mind. After all, I only had $4 invested in the pair of rabbits who were capable of producing many, many more litters. I was told I might get $2 per bunny on a Saturday morning from kids playing on the lawn at the county courthouse square.

These thoughts lasted only a few hours. I was counting rabbits too soon after they'd "hatched." Imagine my horror after school that day when I opened the hutch to feed the rabbits, and the babies—every last one of them—were missing! I told my sad story to all who would listen. My teacher asked what kind of wire I had used. "Should have used half-inch hail wire," he sighed. "My guess is that a cat was able to get its paw through the chicken wire." (How weird, I thought, but then reckoned, from a cat's point of view, this was easier than chasing mice. Sort of like catching fish in a rain barrel.)

It made sense—we had a cat—we called her our "mouser." We noticed that she seemed quite content just to lie around the next couple of days, like out-of-shape old men in front of the television after Christmas dinner....I guess she was also our "rabbiter...." (Critical error number two: When you don't know how to build a rabbit hutch, ask—don't just guess. As Dad said, "If it's worth doing, it's worth doing right." Unless, as he admitted later, there was the convenience of chicken wire lying around, but hail screen would have to be bought....In such a reflective work as this, it seems important to work in a "my dad always said" line. But, it has always seemed to me that such quotes usually are first uttered by famous people, with dads across the ages later latching on to them as their very own.)

◆ ◆ ◆

THANKFULLY, HOPE SPRINGS eternal in freshmen. My hope? There was still time in the freshman year for one more litter....Time seemed an ally. Near year's end, my doe presented me with 10 baby bunnies. Again, dollar signs floated in my head. Hey, it was near Easter; no telling what the bunnies would bring at the feed store, in a pen right next to the colored chicks! Why, youngsters would choose rabbits about every time. I shared my excitement with my teacher. He congratulated me.

Hours later, he took the congratulations back. At evening's feed time, I was below crest-fallen. The doe, perhaps seeing the cat peering through the new hail screen, probably panicked. It appeared she chose to eat the litter before the cat had a chance to do so! My teacher, ever compassionate, told me that sometimes when screwy things happen to the first litter, the doe becomes "mentally warped," and she does strange things to the second litter.... (Critical error number three: When time is of the essence and final grades are close by, always ask the teacher, "Is there anything else I need to watch out for?" I would gladly have stood guard over both litters, by night and by day, if I had even suspected such a dreadful thing might happen.)

Guess what? I made a "B" in agriculture. (I told you the teacher was compassionate.) He also loved funny stories, and didn't we decide the true ones are funniest? The teacher told me he was not going to grade me down for not increasing the rabbit count. But, he warned me to be sure to take care of the buck and doe. (Following the second litter, the doe seemed to have zero interest in having a third bunch of bunnies....)

◆ ◆ ◆

How grateful I was! A "B" is just short of an "A," and plenty "okay" in my book of school life. I was grateful for the chance to prove my worth by really taking care of the old rabbits. I "smooshed" their pellets, made sure their water was fresh and begged my mom for fresh leaf lettuce every chance I got. I was determined to keep mom and pop rabbit healthy! Of course, the rabbit saga continued....What's this? Foreign stuff in poppa rabbit's ear? What is it? Will it spread? Can humans catch it?

It was the last week of school, and I ran, first thing that morning, to file the latest rabbit report with Mr. Wheeler.

"Not to worry," he answered. "Sometimes rabbits get ear canker. It isn't serious; it can be treated with mineral oil a couple of times a day."

Resolved to Raise Rabbits
To be a male freshman at Early High School meant enrollment in "ag" (riculture)—for sure. Most students raised cattle, sheep, goats or hogs. A smattering of us chose rabbits. My experience became a testament for zero population growth.

Mineral oil? Why couldn't it be olive oil, machine oil, 30-weight oil, or any other oil we had around the house? No, the teacher spoke slowly, seeming to carve out each syllable, MIN-ER-AL OIL. Clearly, it had to be this specific oil, one I knew little about, except that it was a remedy people depended on to treat constipation. Wouldn't you know it? We were all out of mineral oil. I told my mother I needed some to treat my rabbits' ears, explaining that Mr. Wheeler insisted that it was the best home remedy. With limited medical knowledge, I didn't admit to Mom that I thought mineral oil was used exclusively as a laxative—it's just not a topic a kid broaches with his mother. No sense embarrassing both of us….

Time was of the essence. Since she was busy cooking dinner, she permitted me to ride my bike to Williams

Store, five miles away. (It was two miles on the dirt road and then three more up the state highway.) A freshman has to do what a freshman has to do. I checked my bike tires, knowing that if I wasn't careful, I would run right over a burr patch, and the next thing I'd hear would be the sickening sound of air spewing out of a punctured tire. Would such an incident make me late to the store? Of course it would, and might delay treatment by a couple of hours. Skillfully, I maneuvered my bike on the country road with nary a puncture. What a relief it was to reach the highway and guide my bike to the edge of the hardtop. I pedaled madly, with dust flying as I skidded to a stop in front of the store. "There is a God," I thought.

Upon arrival, I whispered a two-part prayer—actually, three. First, I thanked the Almighty for safe arrival and deliverance through the burr patches. The other two parts? One was that Mr. Williams, not Mrs. Williams, would be working that day. Mrs. Williams was terribly hard of hearing, and I wasn't eager to yell out that I needed a bottle of MINERAL OIL. My face reddened at the thought that ANYONE would hear my request; I only wanted to say "mineral oil" once. Surely anyone hearing me would assume me to be in a state of constipation. The end of the prayer was that there would be NO OTHER customers in the store, particularly if Mrs. Williams was on duty.

Okay, maybe for just the briefest of seconds, I thought—MAYBE there wasn't a God. I struck out on parts two and three of my prayer. Mr. Williams had gone into town to fetch the mail, and there were four shoppers in the store—all women. "Jeepers," I thought. "Just my luck, having to buy a laxative with five women listening—if Mrs. Williams' efforts could be considered 'listening.'"

Lingering in my mind was my teacher's haunting admonition, "Take good care of your buck and doe." Failing that, I wondered if my prized "B" might melt downward into a "D," or maybe a dreaded "F." It was a serious situation, and again, I realized that a freshman must do what a freshman must do. I walked straight up to Mrs. Williams, shuffling my feet before meekly asking, "Do you have any mineral oil?"

"Have any what?" she answered, leaning over the counter, hoping to hear my plea a little better. "Mineral oil," I repeated. "What kind of oil?" she questioned. Finally, I gutted up with about as much courage as I ever had. Opening my mouth wide, in full surrender, I was determined to speak crisply and with full volume. To heck with it; the syllables could hang out as they would. I said them just the way I remembered my teacher did: "MIN-ER-AL OIL," I fairly bellowed.

Mrs. Williams, serious as church, finally understood. "No, we're all out of mineral oil…." Pausing, she added, as if through a megaphone, "But we've got Ex-Lax, and that's an awful good laxative…." My face felt as if it were on fire. I raced from the store, riding my bike home at warp speed, hang the burrs. As I rode within 100 yards of the house, I even thought of ringing the stupid bell on my bike. "You can use it for emergencies," my mother had said when my granddad—her dad—handed the bell to me as a 12th birthday present. What a "sicko" gift; it was one of those bells pre-schoolers had on their tricycles. It helped them learn to use their thumbs to produce the "brrrrrrng, brrrrng" that may seem loud inside, but is little more than a tinkle outdoors. What was my granddad thinking? It was like getting an ugly painting from relatives. Hideous as the work might be, it still had to be on the wall when they visited. It was that way with the bell on my bike. (My friends would have rolled on the ground laughing if they ever saw the wimpy bell clamped on my bike.) Granddad had visited the day before, so the bell was in place, and I rang it feverishly as I rolled up to the back door. As I had hoped, Mom met me on the porch.

◆ ◆ ◆

IN TEARS, I spilled out a detailed version of what had happened. Mothers are so sympathetic. She understood completely and didn't laugh at the incident—at least not in my presence—until years later.

Calmly, we got in the car. She drove the dozen miles to Brownwood, and Mom, not about to run the risk of embarrassing me twice in the same day with delicate requests for mineral oil to store clerks, suggested that I stay in the car. Ah, that's the very place I wanted to be! Mom marched into the Piggly-Wiggly and returned to the car with a small brown bag. It contained the item so critically needed to perhaps save the life of my rabbit, but, more importantly, to preserve my "B" in agriculture.

Again, God was on His throne; much was right with the world. All's okay, I guess, that ends okay. That's how my freshman year ended. Some kids showed wonderful cattle, even fetching big bucks at the Fat Stock Show in Fort Worth. Same for those showing sheep. And hogs. Me? I started with two rabbits, and finished with two rabbits—healthy fat rabbits I let play on the lawn. Life was sunny side up! There was much to be glad about. I didn't have to wrestle with good-byes to animals I knew soon would be slaughtered and served on restaurant plates. I gagged at the thought of eating my own prized animals. I had those rabbits for several more years. We never even thought of having them as a change from chicken for Sunday dinner. And, rabbit feed wasn't all that expensive.

◆ ◆ ◆

I learned a lot that year....But so did my teacher. The next year, Mr. Wheeler handed out mimeographed sheets telling kids just about everything that could happen to their livestock projects—even step-by-step instructions for building rabbit cages—I mean, hutches. He also learned that grading could be based pretty much on sincere effort, because that's all I had to show for rabbit-raising. Oh, and the livestock judge. Dick claims to have learned a major lesson: Never pretend to be someone you're not. He said that was the only rabbit competition he ever judged. For years afterward, he confessed to having nightmares about asking kids to "reverse their rabbits."

Oh, I learned another mighty important lesson! It was that most things are not worth being embarrassed about. In the years since, many is the time I've entered stores, head held high, to buy mineral oil or whatever, not caring if Mrs. Williams was the clerk, or who might be listening....(I draw the line, though, on going to a woman doctor, unless I'm really sick, and she's the only doctor around.)

◆ ◆ ◆

ONE LAST THOUGHT: When I told my teacher about my efforts to buy a bottle of mineral oil, he reddened. His face was beyond red. His eyes filled with tears—the kind you get when you laugh until you can't catch your breath. We thought he was going to have a smothering spell for sure. After several minutes, he closed his book and tried vainly to control himself. He couldn't, so he dismissed the class 20 minutes early. It was the only time I ever remember getting out of class early, except maybe for P.E. I still prize that "B" on my freshman report card, and consider it something of a gift. And I am thankful for a compassionate teacher who loved life, and kids and jokes, and was a full-fledged participant in a 100% true funny story. They ARE the funniest! You just can't go wrong with a chicken or rabbit story—neither is lousy, true or false!

◆ ◆ ◆

(CRITICAL ERROR NUMBER four: Actually, I averted this error. I refer to the *Holy Bible,* where, in Ecclesiastes 3:1, we are reminded, "To everything there is a season." Even though a trike bell on my bike is a bitter memory, I did NOT ditch the bell. My granddad is long since gone. I know he meant no ill. Besides, it is a strong reminder of a man who had such a positive impact on my life. In a couple of years, when my own grandson lights up the room with a smile seldom equaled—the kind a kid flashes when he first learns to pedal his tricycle—the bell will be in place, clamped right there on the bar by his thumb, so he can make all the "brrrrrng, brrrrng" sounds he wants. But, I've circled the date to make sure when Ben's thoughts turn to bicycles, the trike bell will long since have been put away....)

One absolutely last thought: Riney Jordan, a wonderful friend of more than 40 years who also likes to splash around in the great sea of past experiences, has advised me to share my rabbit-raising story with the people who do advertising for MasterCard, kinda/sorta/maybe like:

Rabbits: $5
Hutches (or cages): $10
Story About a Freshman Ag Project: PRICELESS!

◆ ◆ ◆

Chapter Three

Point A to Point B

What a difference a few decades make as we consider getting from place to place! In the early years, choices were few. Most of the people I knew drove older cars or pick-ups. In the case of my family, it was a pick-up; Dad used it in his work for Central Texas Gas Company. It also had personal use, and there was just enough room for me as a third member of the family. When another adult rode with us, I was relegated to riding in the back of the truck, often with my little brother, Fred. Our dog, Prince, loved to ride back there, too—his front paws on the side of the truck, his gaze ever forward. There were dollops of "dog drool" to be dodged if we were behind him....

Oh, there were other ways of getting around. There was decent bus service from Brownwood to Abilene, San Angelo, Austin and Fort Worth/Dallas, and passenger trains rolled through town, linking Brownwood with San Angelo and Fort Worth. The passenger rail service ended soon after World War II, and not too long after that, more parcels than people went by bus.

Twice each day, my thoughts went skyward when I heard the sounds of the "Blue Goose," a twin-engine aircraft from Fort Worth that made short hops to Brownwood, Abilene, San Angelo and beyond. I don't think that during my youth I knew anyone who PERSONALLY flew on the Trans Texas Airways commuter, but every kid I knew dreamed of flying. Heck, most of my friends had never even ridden a train, including me, and only a few had ever seen an airplane up close.

(In later years, I often flew commercially from the Brownwood Airport to Dallas/Fort Worth, but on a scaled-down commuter plane far smaller than the one I remembered from my youth. In fact, I was sometimes the only passenger, and an important lesson was learned: Never buy potato chips from a vending machine at an airport where the average boardings are three per day....)

MANY RELATIVES AND friends, in those 40's and 50's days, gave little thought about getting from Point A to Point B. As they put it, "We thumbed it." Youth of today's generation would be dumb-struck at 1) knowing what "thumbing it" means, and 2) practicing the same.

"Thumbing it," quite simply, was hitch-hiking. There were more Jericho Roads in those days, and, while there likely were fewer men who fell among thieves back then, there were many hitch-hikers on the roads. They had their thumbs out, in effect begging to ride with passing motorists. With times more carefree, trust at a high level, and a prevailing Christian compulsion to help folks out, "thumbers" had little trouble getting rides.

Relatives getting to our house, though, realized that getting from Brownwood to the "turn-off" was always easy. Not so easy were the two miles remaining on the dirt road. Their decision to "thumb it" our way for a visit depended on how much they wanted to see us, how hungry they were for my mother's homemade biscuits (which she made from scratch AT LEAST twice daily) and/or how "broke" they were.

My granddad (Mom's father) and several of her brothers often landed at our house, sometimes for several days. Often my uncles would forget their "smokes" (cigarettes), and would pay exorbitant prices for relief before they had full-blown nicotine fits. I was the black-marketer who usually had a pack hidden away, never for personal use, but to extract huge profits from desperate relatives. I was able to sell the cigarettes, one at a time, for ludicrous amounts. When a guy craves a smoke, is more than an hour away from a store and is "thumbing it," money means little, never mind how stale the cigarettes might be.

I never heard of a rental car until college years or later. When it was time to leave home (actually, beyond time), it was time to round up my earthly belongings for a 330-mile move to Alpine, Texas, where I was to be Instructor of Journalism and Director of College Information (two lines on my business card) for Sul Ross State University. Alpine is deep in Southwest Texas; it has been said that if the world were square, Alpine would be one of the corners. You hardly ever heard Sul Ross mentioned without a reference to Dan Blocker; that's where he went to school. (This fact seemed to legitimatize the school. Blocker, on NBC's blockbuster TV show, "Bonanza," was the heralded "Hoss" Cartwright, watched by tens of millions of people in most parts of the world each week.)

I was 25 years of age, two years removed from graduation at Howard Payne University, and had a considerable preoccupation with getting from Point A to Point B. In what seemed to be seven very short years, I had purchased six vehicles—almost one a year—including three new ones. The first, a '49 Nash Ambassador purchased in 1957, when I was 20 years old, looked something like a bloated coffin. Following were a '54 Ford, a butane-burning '56 Oldsmobile, a '60 Plymouth, a '61 Mercury and finally, the '63 Buick. Ah, only in America are unending car payments assumed to be a way of life! This is a given in this land of the mortgaged and home of the unafraid....

◆ ◆ ◆

AT SUL ROSS, I was to get free furnished housing if I would be a dormitory director, which, of course, I would. Still, I had accumulated a few things—things that would not begin to fit into the big Buick. Obviously, a trailer was needed to get the things from Brownwood to Alpine, Point A to Point B.

I went down to the rental place, and froze at the prospect of paying $40 to pull a trailer one-way to Alpine. (It was a "Go West, Young Man" time in history, so I figured they should pay ME to pull the trailer further west for them....) Not so.

"Uncle" Cecil Holman, the African-American undertaker in Brownwood who was one of several mentors during my college years, listened to my woeful tale. "Mr. Berries, (that's what he always called me), I think I've got a deal for you that will make you throw rocks at the rental place," he said. He had a friend who had an old trailer for sale for just $30. "Just been used around Palestine over in East Texas," he emphasized.

Upon seeing it, I figured he had the part about Palestine right, but maybe it was in the Holy Land, not East Texas. It was a rickety-looking four-wheeler with what Uncle Cecil claimed were "may-pop" tires. (The kind that may pop at any time, he warned.) Still, it seemed a good deal, and Uncle Cecil was able to pick up a spare for me—just to be safe—for $5 more. The plan, of course, was to use the trailer, then sell it for a profit upon arrival in Alpine....

◆ ◆ ◆

"THERE'S MANY A SLIP 'twixt the cup and the lip,'" Shakespeare penned, and was this ever to become obvious to me! Early on the day of departure, trailer loaded and hooked behind my shiny new Buick, I thought about how out of place the old trailer must have looked—old and new hooked together. I was thankful that an Alpine friend already had offered a place to store it until its sale. Heaven forbid many people seeing it!

Ten miles beyond San Angelo, one of the "may pop" tires did. I stopped the car, and was in the process of putting on the spare tire when a college chum, Don Abbott, stopped to render aid. I explained that everything was under control, and said the same thing a bit later when a courteous state trooper offered assistance. They both recommended my going back into San Angelo to get another spare. Sounded good to me.

I had driven just a few miles back toward San Angelo when I saw something racing across the field to my left. Spotting it coincided with the metal-against-pavement sound emitting from the trailer hub. (When the helpers stopped to offer assistance, I got out of sequence. The lug bolts were on, but not tightened. I had simply forgotten this important task.) They had come loose, and there I was. Luckily, I was able to find the wheel in the cotton patch, but I had no lug bolts to secure it on the hub. They were no doubt scattered along the way....

Eureka! I thought of the old joke of the man whose wheel flew off on the highway near a mental institution. Puzzled as to what he might do, he heard a resident yell, "Hey, Mister, take one bolt off each of the other wheels, and 'make do' until you can get to town." The traveler was grateful, wondering aloud why a man with such a mind would be in a mental institution. "Because I'm crazy, not stupid," the resident answered.

So, I removed some lug bolts from the other wheels, tightened them up, and drove slowly back into town. It was a Sunday, and it took a while to find a service station open. When I did, the man working was pumping gas, fixing flats and repairing fan belts. I was about fifth in line, and he laughed when I asked if he had any used tires.

"Used?" he questioned. "Of course not. You've got a rare wheel size there, buddy, but luckily I think I've got one new one. It'll cost you $15."

I gulped and did some quick addition. Yep, I now had $50 in it—$10 more than a nice, reliable rental trailer would have cost. Thankfully, though, I found the needed tire, and just three hours later, it was ready to go. I was 100 miles down the road, with 230 miles to go. Still, I was in fair shape mechanically, it seemed, and I headed west again....

◆ ◆ ◆

UPON REACHING FORT Stockton, still more than an hour from Alpine, I watched the sun dying in the west. Before I could get melancholy, and maybe write down some nice poetry, reality set in again: There were no lights on the trailer. Another cost must be added: $15 for a motel room for the night. Arriving in Alpine the next day, I unloaded, facing just one last move for the trailer—to my friend's garage for safekeeping until it was sold. I felt less certain about making a profit, but still figured I might come out on the deal with little or no cost for the move. Wrong! In downtown Alpine, the trailer fell off the axle. As it splintered against the pavement, its value plunged to zero. I realized the $40 trailer the rental people offered would have been a bargain indeed.

A few days later, I told my sad story to George Dolan, whose THIS IS WEST TEXAS column about Texans' antics appeared daily in the FORT WORTH STAR-TELEGRAM for more than a quarter-century. He howled with laughter about my misadventure and thanked me for his next day's column. Later the next day, I welcomed a call from the U-Haul headquarters in Grand Prairie, Texas. The folks there were likewise amused by the column, and seized on it as a testimonial possibility. They said if I would sign an advertisement pledging always to rent from U-Haul in the future, they would send me a $100 check—more than enough to pay my moving expenses. Hooray! It turned out that I would actually make a few bucks on the move....

◆ ◆ ◆

Three travel experiences involving public transportation come to mind where I was the only passenger, and the situations involved a plane, a train and a bus. On the train, I wasn't the only passenger, but I was the only one in the Pullman car. During a weeklong tour in Kansas, I spoke at banquets nightly. With two nights remaining, I turned in my rental car in western Kansas, figuring I could ride the train most of the night to reach my final stop in Topeka. I had never ridden in a Pullman car and thought this might be the perfect time for such an experience. An attentive porter listened as I mentioned a concern of being asleep upon reaching Topeka, possibly waking up much later to learn that I had missed my getting off place, perhaps then several hours away from Topeka.

"Mister, you ain't got no problems," he laughed. "You are the only one on this car, and it will be 'turned loose' on a sidetrack in Topeka. You can sleep all day if you want to!" I slept little, what with the constant shaking of the train, but did fall asleep when the car was "turned loose." In fact, I slept until noon, then decided to walk around the depot before an afternoon nap and the evening speech. Near the side track was a pay phone booth. Someone left a pizza coupon in the booth, so I decided to "eat in" back in my private Pullman car. I placed my pizza order, assuring the lady that it should be delivered to "my car," hinting that it was, indeed, my car! In fact, I carefully explained that the delivery guy should rap on the LEFT door, since the right one was for credit card purchases! (I wanted to cause some real head-scratching at the pizza place, where they probably figured they'd heard it all.…) Sure enough, a pizza delivery boy appeared, stepping tentatively across the tracks. He glanced left, then right, then left again, rapping on the door. I paid him and left the door cracked as he walked away. I heard him say, "This is the first time I ever delivered pizza to a train!"

◆ ◆ ◆

On another occasion, when oil prices went south in the 80's, airline service to West Texas was curtailed. There were fewer flights, and several airlines previously serving such cities as Midland and Odessa scaled down to much smaller aircraft. I was scheduled to fly on Continental Airlines on what happened to be the last big bird used on the route. I was shocked to be the only passenger; the other 150 or so seats were empty. There were a pilot and co-pilot up front, and four flight attendants kept me company in the cabin. When one did her spiel about safety procedures, she started laughing when she got to the part about "if you have an infant with you, please place the oxygen mask around your face before placing it on the infant.…" I had no infant! Soon there was a card game going, with flight attendants playing, taking turns bringing refreshments. It was a "heady" experience until the pilot told me after landing the aircraft that they had to pick up several people for a final flight from Midland to

Dallas, whether it had arrived empty, full, or with just one person....

◆ ◆ ◆

FINALLY, THE BUS. While at Howard Payne, I was invited to speak at a church banquet 100 miles away in San Angelo. A musical group from the university also was invited. The only snag in the plan was that the quartet had no transportation, so I offered them my car. I decided to ride the bus to San Angelo a few hours early, getting in visits with a couple of donors before the kids arrived. Boarding the bus in Brownwood around noon, I was the ONLY passenger. The bus made stops in Bangs, Santa Anna, Coleman and Ballinger, but only to drop off and pick up freight. When I got off the bus in San Angelo, the driver continued his route out west with zero passengers. I guess drivers whose only company is freight get mighty lonely. We enjoyed lively conversation for the two hours, and he started it! We totally disregarded the sign posted at the front of the bus: Do Not Talk to Driver While Coach is in Motion. We talked plenty....

◆ ◆ ◆

UPON ARRIVAL IN Snyder in the spring of 1980, I was delighted to learn that an annual activity included attendance at the annual convention of the American Association of Community and Junior Colleges. Within a week after taking the job, Brenda and I were on our way to Washington, D.C. with 14 trustees and spouses in tow.

None of us will likely ever forget the "going and coming" trips. I drove the new school mini-bus on the four-hour trip to Dallas/Fort Worth International Airport without incident. Life got interesting soon after take-off, though. About 20 minutes into the flight, the nose of the plane dipped downward, emergency lights came on, and oxygen masks dropped. It was a sold-out flight, and just one mask failed to drop—mine! Brenda was huffing and puffing when I tugged at her arm to see if she would share her oxygen. (Forget the part about being instructed to "secure the mask on your face, and continue to breathe normally.") She shook her head sideways, not even willing to pull the mask away for the short time it would have taken for her to verbally say, "No." I summoned a flight attendant; she was ashen-faced, and used a screwdriver to open the door that released an oxygen mask for me....

The plane landed without incident in Oklahoma City. A light had indicated that the cabin was depressurizing, so the pilot decided to land the plane at the first opportunity, and this was OKC. (It was comforting as we deplaned to hear the flight attendants remarking that none of them ever had been on flights where the oxygen masks were released....)

American Airlines rolled out another plane and within an hour, our flight to Washington resumed. Soon, flight attendants were moving about the cabin serving lunch. Brenda was served first, and the flight attendant returned to the galley to get more food. "You don't mind if I go ahead and eat, do you?" my wife asked. "I didn't mind if you went ahead and lived; why should I mind if you go ahead and eat?" I deadpanned.

Five days later, it was time to leave DC for the return trip home. The plane's departure was delayed by several hours, and it was necessary for the pilot to skirt around thunderstorms en route. Upon arrival at D/FW, we were greeted by torrential rains, still facing a four-hour trip to Snyder. By this time, night had fallen, so we had dinner, then started the trip. Let me clarify: I started the trip. Everyone else was dozing as the clock moved on toward midnight. The rain continued relentlessly, and within a couple of hours, the length of the day and the continuous "swish-swish-swish" of the windshield wipers made remaining alert problematic.

Suddenly, I felt the left front wheel of the bus hit gravel to the left of the pavement, and I saw the lights of an oncoming truck flashing on and off as the driver did all he could to get my attention. He got it! I regained control of the bus, and I don't think anyone on board did more than blink during the remainder of the trip to Snyder. The near-miss got my attention; why, I think I could have made it to El Paso! By this point, I am sure board members were wondering just what kind of guy they had hired as their president. A few days later, I drove past the place where I dozed off. I was shocked to see vast expanses for several miles either side of that spot with deep ditches. How fortunate we were, for the short distance I dozed, to have a wide shoulder along side....

Sterling Simms is recalled as a prime example of the possible danger between Point A and Point B—even if they are only a few blocks apart. I spotted this Howard Payne freshman on the parking lot one day. I was en route to the service station to get my car serviced, and asked Sterling if he would drive my wife's car and pick me up after the drop-off. "Sure, Doc," he responded, telling me after we returned home that he was surprised I would let him drive a car. "Why wouldn't I, Sterling?" I questioned. His answer was immediate: "I don't have a driver's license!" (The youngest of 10 children, Sterling had come to college with just a bike, but it never occurred to me that he had never learned to drive a car.) The trip from the campus to the service station became his first lesson!

A few years earlier, the Brownwood Coliseum filled for my inauguration. One chair, however, remained empty. It was reserved for a young man who very much wanted to be present. His name? Trey Martin. (He is the son of classmates Bunny and Mary Etta Martin.) At the time he was 24 years of age and already a pilot for Muse Air, flying DC-9's around the country. He arrived in Dallas in plenty of time to rent a car and make the three-hour drive to Brownwood. One catch: Because he was under 25 years of age, no rental company would provide him a car. What irony! He was qualified to fly a large airliner, but not qualified to rent a car—not even a little bitty one. He had just piloted a DC-9 hundreds of miles to Dallas. Unable to rent a car, he missed the inauguration at Point B by 150 miles....

Chapter Four

A Family of My Own

It was "once over lightly" for most duties at Sul Ross, where my responsibilities were as varied and disjointed as my dad's had been at May Schools! But, I had a contract, read it carefully and signed it—happy to have a job that seemed to provide enough remuneration to meet all my needs. (Usually it did, but many times in the coming years, I borrowed no-interest money from my folks, who somehow always had some stuck back.)

Upon arrival in Alpine, I could easily have surrendered to homesickness. Dr. Newman had predicted that "I wouldn't make it three months," and for a few days, I thought he might be right! When one has lived 25 years with parents, 330 miles is quite a stretch into a far country....I missed them, I missed my Brownwood friends, and certainly I missed both the BROWNWOOD BULLETIN and Radio Station KBWD, two media that had been big parts of my life for several years. My folks saved the BULLETINS, sometimes mailing them to me 10 or 12 at a time.

But, KBWD was only a memory, or so I thought. This little radio station, broadcasting with a thousand watts of power, was barely heard beyond the county lines most directions from Brownwood. At night, power was reduced to 250 watts; why some light bulbs were stronger! A few nights after arriving in Alpine, driving aimlessly around town, I wistfully punched the station button still marked "KBWD" on my car radio. Could it be that I heard a familiar voice? Yes, it was the voice of Dallas Huston and the broadcast of a Brownwood Lions baseball game! I simply could not believe it. The radio signal from KBWD rarely exceeded 30 miles at night, yet on this night, it was reaching 11 times that far, and fairly booming in.

It was a phenomenon not to be explained. When I drove forward a few yards on the loop road, the signal faded, then disappeared completely. I backed up, and it came in again, but if I backed too far, static took over....When I again found the very best spot on the road to pick up KBWD, I realized I was directly under an electric power line in front of Alpine Country Club. Huston, a longtime friend, is as good a sports broadcaster as has ever come down the pike. So on game nights during my four years in Alpine, I would park my car on the side of the road, under the power lines, in front of the country club, and enjoy his coverage of Lion and Yellow Jacket games. I don't think I ever picked up the station's signal again, despite efforts from other miscellaneous West Texas locations. But I could always count on crystal clear reception at this one spot in Alpine. Ah, I just couldn't place a value on this important link with home....

◆ ◆ ◆

I was immersed in my work at Sul Ross; it just never all got done. There were classes to teach, both general and sports news to write, and an honors dorm to monitor. (Thankfully, I didn't bother students and they didn't bother me, so maybe the dorm job shouldn't be listed as a duty, but it did provide free housing.) During the two years I lived there, not one of the 24 residents ever mentioned anything about my being the director….

(A year later, I had my own private dorm during two years of summer study at the University of Texas in Austin. During the long term, it provided housing for about 90 young men. In the summer, Concordia, a small Lutheran school just a few blocks from UT, kept it cool for the dorm director who chose to travel all summer long. Therefore, I was the building's only occupant, paying Concordia $30 monthly. I never once met the dorm director, Dr. Norbert Dettmann, until we were colleagues a decade later at Tarrant County Junior College in Fort Worth.)

For many years, I half expected to get some sort of "surcharge" for electricity costs to cool an entire dormitory; I am sure they were significant even back then, and I am certainly glad they chose to have the dorm cooled for Dr. Dettmann, just in case he dropped in during the summer!

During the Sul Ross years, I also was Sports Information Director of the Lone Star Athletic Conference. This additional responsibility provided another $100 per month for duties that included dispensing mountains of information and statistics for all sports of the eight member schools.

◆ ◆ ◆

During my third year there, the prettiest, most poised and delightful student I ever saw enrolled in my journalism class. Her name was Brenda Pack. I was in the Lions' Club and the Chamber of Commerce with her father, V. V. Pack, who managed the local Safeway Store. Her mother worked in the Alpine Public Library. Brenda was a marvelous student, as popular as anyone on campus and the recipient of numerous honors, including basketball sweetheart. Soon after meeting her, it occurred to me what a "find" she would be for my brother. She's only a couple of years his junior, and I started trying to think of ways I might arrange a meeting. Surely he would want to meet her just as soon as he could make a trip out to Alpine.

From time to time, people would see Brenda and me together (usually with others present) and make some comment like, "Hey, Don, why don't you see if Brenda would go out with you?" Invariably, a stock response—one I had learned from my best friend and later to be our best man, Groner Pitts, affable Brownwood funeral director—went like this: "Gee, I would if I were just 10 years younger!" One day during such a scenario, Brenda's response shook me like none other during our more than 35 years of marriage! "If you were 10 years younger, you might be too young," she said, showing more courage and boldness than I thought she possessed!

I couldn't sleep. I couldn't eat. I couldn't wait to call her dad to see if it was okay to ask her out. He said he didn't know if she would go, but he wouldn't mind if I gave it a shot....

My next call was to Brenda. I asked her if she would like to go to Odessa with me the following Saturday. She agreed! There, I would be covering the West Texas Relays, but following the meet, we could have a nice dinner before driving the 140 miles back to Alpine. That was March 19, 1966. My car broke down on the late night trip home. We were able to catch a ride on the back of a pick-up truck back to Fort Stockton, where I borrowed a car from a friend, and we arrived back in Alpine around 5:30 a.m. I was sure her folks would be frantic. What good luck! We woke them up! After our first date, there were few days that we did not see each other.

◆ ◆ ◆

We were engaged in May, and on August 12, 1966, were united in marriage—146 days after our first date. It was a "stormy start," with thunder and lightning in Alpine on our wedding day. In fact, lightning struck the church organ, so all music for the wedding turned out to be a cappella. The marriage has spanned 36 years, and Brenda's role as the wife of a college administrator, after-dinner speaker and sports nut has no doubt been challenging.

In every way, she has been as near perfect a life partner as one could pray for, and an even better mother! When we were married, Brenda was not yet 20 years of age, and lacked one year of college. I was almost 29. She was mature far beyond her years and continues to hold her own. I'm still trying to catch up!

One year later, when she completed her B.A. degree at Sul Ross, I was offered the position of Director of Community Relations at the new Tarrant County Junior College. The Chancellor of the institution was Dr. Joe B. Rushing, who was Executive Vice President of Howard Payne during my early years there. The job would pay

$12,000 annually, and my primary task was to work toward a positive public image—to keep us in the news and off the front page!

And Then, It Was 2000
This picture was made in 2000—my 40th and final year of work in higher education. Brenda and I observed our 34th wedding anniversary the same year, and moved to Fort Worth in August of 2000.

Brenda would seek a public school teaching job, and we were off to Fort Worth in August of 1967. She taught English and Biology at Arlington Heights High School. In addition to my work for TCJC, I took doctoral classes at North Texas State University two nights each week. This regimen for the next seven years led to a Ph.D. degree in Higher Education Administration in 1973. (My brother Fred received his doctorate the same night, having caught up with me by working toward the degree for two years on a fulltime basis.)

◆ ◆ ◆

Brenda was pregnant with our first of three daughters in the fall of 1969, so her teaching career ended just two and a half years after it began. We both were resolved to her being a full-time mom, and she has done so magnificently.

Julie (now Mrs. Bryan Choate) was born July 2, 1970; then came Jana (Mrs. Kyle Penney) on March 20, 1973, and finally Jeanie (Mrs. Ryan McDaniel) on July 31, 1975. Our daughters have been the lights of our lives since each entered the world....The church has been central to the lives of our family. Emphases on church, family, school and work have worked for us!

There have been tons of joy and ounces of regret. I started a public speaking career in addition to my "day job" when Brenda's teaching ended, and the extra money helped finance braces, piano lessons and weddings for each daughter! All three were wonderful students; how we thank God for each of them. Now, all of them are public school educators. And, what a wonderful event occurred last year! Julie and Bryan gave us our first grandchild—Benjamin David Choate—on May 22, 2001.

Each of our daughters has distinctive qualities, but a common thread is their talent as pianists. All three took piano lessons for 8-10 years, and all three were piano accompanists for the choirs of Brownwood High School, as well as for numerous church vocal groups. One day, a senior adult woman in our church called the house, asking if Jana, then a high school senior, could play an opening hymn for the senior adults the next Sunday. I responded that Jana was to be away on Sunday, but that I felt Jeanie, a high school freshman and likewise talented on the piano, would be happy to play. The caller said she would "think about it," then get back with us. Luckily, I answered the phone when she called back the next day explaining that she "just didn't feel like Jeanie was quite seasoned enough to play hymns the way the senior adults would like!" (Had Brenda answered the phone, she wouldn't have railed at the woman, but no doubt smoke would have poured from her ears!)

◆ ◆ ◆

EARLY ON, JULIE had a strong interest in horses. When Groner Pitts heard this, he sprang to action. Remember, he is the consummate court jester and practical (or even worse, impractical) joker....On Christmas eve in 1977, when Julie was just seven years of age, our doorbell rang. I went to the door, and there stood Pitts, holding the reins of Trixie, a beautiful three-year-old horse. He handed me the reins, said, "Merry Christmas" to Julie, and drove away. There I stood, stunned at the very least, and wondering what to do with a horse in a traditional neighborhood with an ordinary home and an average backyard? I figured that the only sensible thing to do that night was to put the horse in the backyard....The next morning, I learned first-hand why horses have to have more space....Horse manure adorned much of the yard....

Thankfully, friends a couple of miles away with small acreage agreed to keep Trixie, and as often as possible, I drove Julie out to ride her horse. I unfolded a yard chair, catching up on newspaper reading, staying close by just in case I was needed.

◆ ◆ ◆

In 1980, Julie was 10, Jana, 7 and Jeanie, 5, and the thought of rearing the children in a small town appealed to both Brenda and me. With doctoral degree in hand and 14 years experience at TCJC, I applied for the presidency of Western Texas College in Snyder and was hired.

Driving our aged Lincoln and pulling a horse trailer packed with our belongings, we made the move to Snyder in several similar trips. On the last one, we were driving into the teeth of a brisk wind. Upon leaving Abilene, I looked at the gas gauge, figuring we had just enough gas to drive the 70 remaining miles to Snyder. I forgot that we were facing a headwind, and that the car was pulling a loaded trailer. About five miles outside Snyder, the car sputtered to a stop. What to do? It occurred to me that the last item I stuck in the trailer was a bicycle. I left the family in the car, unloaded the bike, rode to Snyder, got a can of gas and returned to the car....

The college provided housing, and we found a place to keep Trixie. Jana, thinking she, too, was supposed to like horses, played the part, so we bought her a pony named Kiowa. We now had two horses to look after....A few years later, after Kiowa tossed riders a few times, only Julie remained a horse lover. Kiowa was sold, and when Julie became busy with high school, Trixie likewise went to the only bidder....(I felt like the guy who had a herd of horses to sell, and took a $100 check for the last two horses he owned. The check bounced. "It was still a good deal," he maintained....)

Parents rarely write down all the precious and/or hilarious things their offspring say and do, but Brenda and I have our share of such memories. Many of them are written down; in some cases, too much is written. Sometimes children take note of such entries, particularly in baby books. Brenda, noting the exact date that Jeanie began walking, wrote that she was "a little slower" than the other two....In the intervening years, Jeanie has kidded her mom regularly that too much should not be expected of her—after all, she is a little slower than the other two....

All three girls are honor graduates of Brownwood High School. I don't recall EVER talking to the girls about improving their grades at school. They were already improved! (Discipline wasn't much my thing, either. I occasionally had words with each of them on disciplinary matters, but when I had words, their mother had paragraphs....)

WHEN I WAS named president of Howard Payne in late 1985, it occurred to me that there was a chance that our daughters would meet some fine young men there, and that our sons-in-law might well be from HPU. We made "deals" with each daughter upon high school graduation. Brenda and I suggested that at least two years be spent at a Baptist university. We would finance these costs, as well as the final two years at the schools of their choosing. (We figured once they got started, they would want to finish up at the same school.) We also explained that if an out-of-town university were chosen, we would be able to provide a three-or four-year-old car. If, however, Howard Payne should be their choice, a current model car would be provided for each....

Lights of Our Lives
Our three daughters, Julie, Jana and Jeanie, all of whom are Howard Payne University graduates, now serving in Aledo, Midway and Sanger Public Schools, respectively.

And it worked! The girls all chose Howard Payne, and all majored in education, preparing to become public school teachers. They have expressed repeatedly how delighted they are to have made the decision to stay in Brownwood to go to school. They were sad only at holiday times, when other students had road trips home, and they were already there....

No, they didn't live at home during college. All three lived in the women's dormitory. At dozens of speeches, I have claimed to well understand how parents feel when their children go away to college. "How well I remember the day Julie drove off to college," I began, words choking a bit, and trying to produce a few tears. "We loaded up her car, kissed her on the cheek, then watched her drive away. My wife and I waved....then watched her car stop, two blocks up the street, where a host of students helped her move her things into the dorm...."

◆ ◆ ◆

The son-in-law acquisition theory was almost 100% wrong. On June 11, 1994, Julie married Bryan Choate, a graduate of Liberty University. Later, on June 7, 1997, Jana was married to Kyle Penney, a graduate of Baylor University. We only recently paid off the third wedding. On July 7, 2001, Jeanie was married to Ryan McDaniel, a graduate of Wayland Baptist University. It was Ryan, however, who kept me from missing the mark a full 100%. He attended HPU for a year! Our sons-in-law are wonderful Christian gentlemen....even though they graduated elsewhere!

◆ ◆ ◆

Chapter Five

Bring On the Good Deals!

One of life's brightest moments, I believe, is when both parties in a trade believe they made a killing—you know, a really good deal! That's probably the way it was back in 1626, when the shrewd Dutch traders swapped beads and other goods with the Delaware Indians for what is now the Manhattan Island. "We can always get some more beads, and this is going to be some kind of real estate one day," the traders may have thought. The Indians couldn't wait to replace their bear-teeth necklaces with the shiny beads, thus setting new fashion standards for tribes everywhere. Perhaps they were snickering that they knew where plenty more land was..., and probably their allergies would be better there..., and there certainly wouldn't be as many foreigners to deal with....

Both sides were satisfied. I can identify with either. No doubt this shrewd trading acumen pre-dated the manufacturing of tires to kick, and deals were being made all the way back to Abraham in Biblical times. Looking back on a lifetime of accepting many good deals, the ones I thought best went south—some over a period of many years—some overnight!

◆ ◆ ◆

A COLLEGE CHUM, now the Rev. Marion Fonville, was always coming across good deals, and most of the time, he let me in on them. Since he found several good used cars for me over the years, I forgave him for some other deals that were as bogus as could be!

One day, back in 1971, he offered me a "can't miss" tip. The Eisenhower silver dollars had just started circulation, and he had it on good authority that in just a few years, they would likely triple in value. He advised me to buy up as many as I could get my hands on. A friendly cashier at my bank watched for them, stashing the silver dollars away, knowing that within a day or two, I would be in to trade paper Washington dollars that seemed certain to be worth just that—face value—many years up the road.

Over the next several months, I accumulated $600 in the silver dollars. At that point, I hadn't actually "put the pencil" to the cost of this good deal. Storing this prize in a safe place required the rental of one of the bank's larger safe deposit boxes. What the heck, I thought. As much money as I'm bound to make, this yearly rental is but a small hiccup in the swallows of life....

The years rolled by...moves were made to Snyder and to Brownwood...bank box rentals were paid annually...a quarter-century passed. From time to time, I checked on the value of the Eisenhower silver dollars. From the day I purchased the first one until the time I started disposing of them, the value had increased by a nickel to $1.05. Brenda and I eventually decided to give 200 silver dollars to each daughter the first Christmas following her marriage. There, that was that. Now, I surrender—yet again—to rationalization. After all, we needed a safe deposit box. But in reality, one six times smaller would have been fine—except that it wouldn't have held even half of the silver dollars. I once calculated that $600 in simple savings would have compounded to more than $3,000 in 25 years, but Marion assured me it was a good deal....Back on Manhattan Island, he would have been one of the Indians....

◆ ◆ ◆

SOON AFTER BEGINNING the silver dollar search, I ran across an interesting item in the classified ads. (For years, I've been fascinated by unlikely items people sell, and the intriguing descriptions some of them have. One ad for a bedroom suite claimed it was made from "naughty pine.") The FORT WORTH STAR-TELEGRAM ad was for stuffed animals. One of the shops at Six Flags Over Texas amusement park was liquidating, with the animals—the whole lot—offered for pennies on the dollar. Remembering that Fonville's church youth were looking for a fund-raising project, I called him to let him know of the stuffed animals. We both figured the kids could sell the individual animals at a handsome profit. He was busy that day and asked if I would borrow a pick-up and trailer and make the purchase. Of course I would!

That night, Marion called to say he had re-thought the matter and decided the stuffed animals' re-sale might be "iffy," so he suggested I pass on the deal. He was a few hours late. I had already handed about $600 in cash to the happy shop-keeper and returned the pick-up and trailer. Some of the stuffed animals were as big and long as school-age children, and there wasn't enough room in our garage for storage. In fact, some of them were stacked three feet deep in our dining room, thus making the room off-limits, even for walking through. Toddlers can't read off-limits signs, and Jeanie, then eight months old, crawled right in amongst the animals. When we couldn't find her, we started tossing animals aside to retrieve her....

Something had to be done. I ran a small classified ad, and a couple of the animals were sold. I hired a neighborhood youngster to hawk them from the car parked at a busy intersection, getting rid of another dozen or so. But, a couple of hundred remained....As a last resort, I called the SHOPPER, a free publication distributed in the city each week. "New stuffed animals for pennies on the dollar," I had planned for the ad to read. The lady taking the ad stopped me, indicating that it seemed to HER like this would be a good fund-raising project for the youth at HER church! She bought the remaining animals at my cost. We could use our garage and dining room again, as well as better keep up with our three daughters. Who knows? Maybe her youth group did well on the deal; I know I did, just breaking even! This was the closest we ever came to living in a zoo....

Actually, looking for "deals" probably began when decisions had to be made concerning candy purchases in pre-school years. Candies went for 1 to 5 cents each, and I was a sucker for "Guess-Whats" in the early going. This item contained cheap taffy in loosely-wrapped paper. BUT, despite the temptation of buying a much better candy, I usually wound up choosing "Guess-Whats," because each came with a flimsy prize. (Later, there were even better prizes in Cracker Jacks, and those tasted better, too.)

◆ ◆ ◆

AS A JUNIOR in high school, I was pumped with the rest of the nation about the exciting adventure movie the Disney people produced; it was called "Davy Crockett—King of the Wild Frontier." Besides being a box office smash, this was the first movie I recall that produced popular product spin-offs. In this case, replicas of the coon-skin cap worn by Davy Crockett at the Alamo and by Texan Fess Parker, star of the movie, became popular among the younger set. Most were undeterred by the price tag. If memory serves, millions of the caps were sold in stores for $1.98 each.

In a year or so, the rage was waning, but no one told me. Visiting in Fort Worth one day, I spotted a sale on coonskin caps. Regularly $1.98, they were offered for a mere 11 cents each! I couldn't wait to box up all they had—I think it was about three dozen. Immediately, I was the "man with the plan." I would take them back home to Brown County and sell them for 50 cents a piece, thus lining my pockets with several dollars in easy profit. Well, I think my arrival back in Brownwood coincided with the news—already known, no doubt, by most people in the free world—that the coonskin cap rage had run its course. I felt low enough to walk under a bath tub with a fireman's hat on! Few kids could be found who wanted coonskin caps, even for free. I finally tossed several of them into a box, figuring one day our children would come across the box, shriek with delight and immediately don the coonskin caps, probably even wanting to get their pictures made! Wrong again! Julie, at age five, came across the box—as predicted. BUT—she wasn't about to even so much as "touch a yucky dead animal." Put it on HER head? Double yucks. And put the camera away.... Sadly, it was another "good deal" gone south....

The stories could go on—particularly concerning "can't miss" stock market deals. Alas, they are too many, too frequent and yes, even too recent. Let's just say that most of my investments in the stock market have been "sweet chariot stocks." When we buy them, they swing low....But then, sometimes in the most unexpected way, everything comes up roses even when evidence mounts to the contrary....

◆ ◆ ◆

Brenda and I were concluding a car trip in Canada and were en route back to Calgary for the night before our flight home the next morning. Before we left Texas, she urged me to make all hotel reservations, and I agreed. EXCEPT: I figured we would just "wing it" for the night prior to flying out. We could find a room, "only needing one." She did not respond, and such silence does not always mean consent....As we were turned away from hotel after hotel in Calgary, she reminded me of the remark about needing just one room per night—multiple times....

Wee hours were approaching, and flight time was roughly 10 hours away when I heard the "sold out" response at my sixth stop. "Is there a reason why all the hotels are full?" I asked the clerk. "Have you ever heard of the Calgary Stampede?" he asked, explaining that it is the world's largest rodeo. He said it was in full swing, and there wasn't a hotel room to be found within 50 miles of Calgary....

Not satisfied with that answer, I asked about meeting rooms. "We have meeting rooms for as few as 40 or as many as 400 people," the clerk bragged. "Are any available tonight?" I asked. "All of them are," he responded. "Do any of them have sofas that convert to beds?" my questioning continued, and yes, some did. "May I rent one of those?" was my plea.

The clerk, perhaps amused by my persistence, agreed to do so, tossed me a set of sheets and some towels and charged me the regular room rate. We unfolded the sofa bed and readied for a short night's sleep—kidding that if we chose to do so, we *could* have a reception for 38 guests and sleep there, too! Given the shortage of hotel rooms, we no doubt could have rented out each chair to frantic folks like us who would have paid big bucks just to sit at a conference table, lean forward with heads down, and catch a few winks....

◆ ◆ ◆

KING OF THE deal-makers had to be Elmo Letbetter who, in the 1930's, opened Letbetter and Sons Mattress Factory and Furniture Store on the corner of Third and Fisk in Brownwood. He arrived at Howard Payne in the 1920's, perhaps not realizing that he would major in generosity—

and deal-making! That's been the major story of his life—making bargain buys, then giving away whatever he purchased. Most beneficiaries of his generosity have been under-privileged children, projects undertaken by First Baptist Church, kids at Howard Payne University and whatever the Lions' Club took on. (When the Lions' Club had fund-raisers, Elmo usually headed the ticket-selling list, or bought the biggest bundles himself to give away....) A community never knew a more generous person. He used his all-purpose van to take youngsters to church and community events; Elmo, it seemed, was everywhere....

Each fall, when watermelons were at their peak and buyers barely dented the supply, melons started selling for pennies instead of dollars. Farmers were eager to get even token amounts for melons ripening in the final days of summer. It was a fall ritual for Elmo to call my office "just to make sure" Howard Payne students still liked watermelon. "You know they do, Elmo," was my stock response. I knew that within a matter of minutes, Elmo would deliver several dozen melons to the cafeteria where students would enjoy them for the next several days.

One Saturday morning, Elmo called me at home, asking if he could deliver a load of melons there. (I had learned years earlier to say "yes" to most of his requests. To do otherwise might result in a longer answer than I cared to hear, or perhaps the "wrong" answer.) He suggested a watermelon party for students; I congratulated him for this fine idea. We had big groups of students down to the house frequently, and watermelon would be as good a reason as any for a party. We didn't talk about the "when part" and headed for the football game.... I thought no more about the melons—until the third quarter. Then I heard Elmo, who had beelined it to the press box to borrow the public address microphone. "Attention Howard Payne students—President and Mrs. Newbury are having a watermelon party at their home right after the game, so plan to go by for a big slice!" (My wife and I slipped out a few seconds before the game ended to get ready for a couple of hundred students to arrive only minutes later.) They did, and we had a good time....Elmo, of course, didn't attend; we hadn't really expected him. He wanted no credit; he preferred that it be "our show." Besides, he probably was out looking for more good deals....

On another Saturday—this time late in the afternoon—Elmo called to say that he had a 100 dozen doughnuts—if Howard Payne students still liked doughnuts. I assured him that they'd welcome the treats, and he asked me to meet him out on Coggin Avenue. I spotted him right in front of the day-old bread store, quickly assuming that they had a real deal on day-old doughnuts. I was partly right! As we were stacking boxes of doughnuts into my van, I noticed bugs playing tag in several of the boxes. In some, there were enough critters for team sports. (Until this time in his life, Elmo got along pretty well with failing eyesight....He had not, of course, seen anything wrong with the doughnuts.) I never told him, but once I got the doughnuts loaded and showered him with thanks, I drove the pastries straight to the city dump. Then, I went home to watch what was left of the 6 o'clock news....

◆ ◆ ◆

WHEN TV SETS became the rage in Texas, a store in Dallas was operated by "Mad Man Muntz," who bragged that he had the best deals in Texas. For years, people laughed at his commercials where he claimed that he really wanted to give the televisions away, but "my wife won't let me—she's crazy!" I knew Elmo for some 50 years, and in all of that time, he "lived out" Muntz's commercial, without ever implicating his wife. Elmo simply liked to go through life giving things away, and those who didn't, well, maybe they were crazy....

More than once, Elmo read in the newspaper that I would be speaking on such and such date in or near Burnet. "I've got a load of ____ or a bunch of ____ (I never knew what) that I've been trying to get down to the Buckner Children's Home at Burnet. Would you mind making a delivery when you go down there to speak?" Elmo would ask. Again, it was easiest and best to respond, "Of course, Elmo."

◆ ◆ ◆

HENRY AND DENISE Lucht, who owned Brown County's first drive-in theatre, the Sunset, also looked for deals. During the 1950's and 1960's, most movies were booked on a negotiated fee basis, and Mrs. Lucht could wrangle with the best of them to pay the very least figure possible for each movie. Meanwhile, her husband was in the concession stand or somewhere else on the premises stretching resources to the limit.

An inventory that stayed on the edge of absolute minimum was marquee letters. One of my duties was to change the marquee a couple of times a week. To reach the lighted marquee, I had to climb a steel ladder to a two-foot-wide catwalk, perhaps 15 feet off the ground. This was no trick even in nice weather, nor was carrying the basket of letters needed for the new movie titles. I had to be creative. Sometimes there weren't enough "A's," so I learned to turn "V's" upside down, slap an "I" across the middle, and use baling wire to attach the makeshift letters. The letters were big—perhaps 18 inches tall—so you couldn't tell that the improvisations were made unless you looked really close, or perhaps got up on the catwalk (the latter being highly unlikely).

I could know by upcoming movie titles what kind of weather to expect. Most weather was fair in Texas, usually warm (or hot) with gentle breezes. When we showed movies with short titles similar to HUD and E. T., it was almost certain we'd have normal weather. If, however, a cold north wind happened to be in the offing, usually with icy conditions, I could expect to brace myself against the wind, figure on creating several makeshift "A's," try to avoid sliding off the catwalk (or being blown off) and get the titles in place. In these terrible conditions, it would be likely that the double feature titles might be CREATURE FROM THE BLACK LAGOON and LOVE IS A MANY-

SPLENDERED THING, spelled and spaced properly, of course.

I made $2.50 per night, working both features in the ticket booth and/or concession stand. Sometimes in the dead of winter, we might show the last couple of reels for occupants of a lone vehicle only to find that the car didn't move when the screen grew dark. It often turned out that the occupants were asleep, so we were showing 30 minutes or more of the movie with no one watching! Exasperated, I would wake them and send them home....Then, just as I was cranking my motor scooter for the short ride home—into the teeth of a strong north wind—Mrs. Lucht would tack on one last duty for the night: "Go back to the marquee and spell 'splendored' correctly—and be careful on the ice...."

Chapter Six

Go Western Texas College, Young Man

Snyder, Texas, located equidistant between Abilene and Lubbock on U. S. Highway 84, has been chiefly sustained by oil production—far and away its primary economic asset during the second half of the 20th century. Until oil discovery, the community had depended largely on agriculture, specifically cotton. When the oil boom hit in the early 1950's, there was not nearly enough housing. Rental property was fully taken, and tents sprang up all over town. Some disgruntled oil people, unable to find any housing, bought a billboard which was maintained for several years. It read: WELCOME TO SNYDER, TEXAS, WHERE THE OIL FLOWS, THE COTTON GROWS AND THE RENT IS TOO DAMNED HIGH!

With oil flowing, the tax base grew dramatically. Scurry County had a population of some 18,000, with about 2/3 of those people living in the county seat town of Snyder. (Oil transforms "billygoat hills" to "Angora Knolls" when they keep adding zeroes to the tax base.) In Scurry County, values reached some three billion dollars, and suddenly, there were tax monies available for many things—including a new courthouse. Some people liked the old one, so they wound up constructing walls of solid marble around it. Schools were upgraded, but the people wanted more—yes, even a community college! (Two-year schools were the national rage in the early 70's, with an average of a new one opening every week across the nation.) Keep in mind that for most of these improvements, oil companies were bearing the brunt of taxes....

◆ ◆ ◆

ON THE COLLEGE issue, the oil companies balked, arguing that higher education needs were being met by area colleges in Lubbock, Abilene and Big Spring. They fought creation of the Scurry County Junior College District. The oil companies had won a battle, but NOT the war....

Citizens were miffed, moving to the "we don't get mad, we get even" posture. Shortly after the college issue failed, another election was held for a 4,000-seat coliseum. This issue passed, and before long, another election was called to revisit the college issue. This time, proponents prevailed, so the oil companies were forced to underwrite majority costs of both a coliseum and a college....

Dr. Robert Clinton, longtime Snyder school superintendent, was Western Texas College's first president; I was the school's second, beginning work there in 1981. At that time, many two-year schools claimed to be comprehensive institutions, but when I realized the oversight, it occurred to me that WTC might deserve to head the list of what comprehensive two-year schools could be.

Two senior citizen programs were directed by WTC, and the Scurry County Museum was on the campus. A golf course maintenance/management program included operation of a nine-hole golf lay-out that also doubled as a municipal golf course, and drama facilities were shared by the community theatre. The world's largest private collection of Wyeth paintings was on display at the Diamond M Museum downtown, and again, WTC provided management and oversight. There was a long list of community service classes offered throughout the year, and extension classes were offered at a half-dozen communities, some as far as 100 miles away. And, yes, WTC faculty also taught traditional university transfer and numerous technical classes on campus. Now that's comprehensive!

◆ ◆ ◆

There was a strong intercollegiate sports program, and in the 1980's, national championships were won in men's basketball, rodeo and judo. I was always cautious at judo competitions. Why? Because I didn't know when to applaud, or how to determine who won until the official made it clear.

Coaching two national championship teams in men's basketball was Nolan Richardson, who holds a distinction achieved by no other coach in the country. He has won national junior college, NCAA and NIT (National Invitation Tournament) championships, moving from WTC to the University of Tulsa and later to the University of Arkansas, where he coached through the 2001-2002 season....

One of our rodeo guys, Dave Appleton from Australia, was Student Body President, and later was "All-around Cowboy of the Year" on the national professional rodeo circuit....

One year, our basketball team advanced to the National Juco Tournament in Huchinson, Kansas. The family and I drove up, eager to see the Westerners compete. Alas, they lost the opening game, and maybe our "undecorated" car had something to do with it. Before arriving in Hutchinson, our girls insisted on splashing "We're No. 1" and other shoe polish messages on the side and back windows....

As we entered town, our spirits soared when we saw the buntings draped across the streets and lighted marquees and billboards, all welcoming us to Hutchinson and the NJCAA basketball tournament! The tournament also provided front page banner headlines in the local paper. Soon, our spirits drooped when we—like many others entering Hutchinson—were stopped by police. The officer, with an expression of pain, told us that a city ordinance prohibited painted windows on automobiles, and that we would need to stop at a carwash to remove the lettering before going to the game. At once, it occurred to me that chamber of commerce people DO NOT write city ordinances, just like bank loan officers aren't the ones who write the TV ads....It further struck me that for this special week of the year, they might want to waive the ordinance, or just maybe the NJCAA ought to "wave goodbye" to the town....

There were lots of times when I didn't know what to do in that first presidency. But, hey, I was president, and most people thought I did! William B. David, distinguished Fort Worth attorney and HPU alumnus, told me to be slow to react, always carry a bunch of rolled-up papers and practice gazing outward toward the horizon. This, he maintained, is a way to buy time, and he is right—assuming, of course, that parties present are waiting and watching for an answer.

It's a way to "take matters under advisement" until advising folks that you are "taking matters under advisement." (My friend, Dr. Lanny Hall, utilized a similar tool concerning matters he considered irrelevant, or even lower than that, in priority. He would say, "I'll certainly plug your suggestion into the equation," meaning that he would never mention it again if you wouldn't....)

◆ ◆ ◆

DAYS AFTER TAKING office, the Snyder Jaycees called, asking us to ring our chimes in honor of United States hostages being released in Iran. This was a two-tiered news discovery to me—first, to learn that the hostages had been released, and second, to learn that we had chimes! My response was, "If we have chimes, we'll ring them!" The Jaycees assured me that WTC did indeed have chimes....

◆ ◆ ◆

OUR CHILDREN LOVED the golf course. On summer evenings, when golfers were finishing up their rounds, most of the time temperatures dipped down toward pleasantness. We would check out a couple of golf carts, and roll around the cart paths, inspecting the course. The kids got a real kick out of it being their turn to drive, and were on the look-out for prairie dogs, rabbits, birds, frogs and pretty sunsets—NOT course conditions!

I was not, am not, nor ever will be considered a golfer. I sometimes played in annual benefits, like the cancer tournament, but my triple-digit trips around the course were well known. One of my friends said if my golf game were a prize fight, they'd stop it! (Dr. Clinton, before me, had greatly enjoyed the game, often playing several times a week. The view from his office, only a few feet from a green, often set off his "itch" to play a few holes. Now retired at a beautiful golf setting, Lakeway (near Austin), he maintains that golf is "not nearly as much fun on your own time!"

◆ ◆ ◆

WTC had just one dormitory, housing 196 students. Others lived in Snyder or commuted from nearby communities, farms, ranches and oil fields. When I mention that it was a co-ed dorm, eyes always roll. Well, it wasn't THAT KIND of co-ed dorm. It just meant that men lived on two of the floors and women on the other two....And the twain never met (that we know of)....

Early on, I emphasized the importance of scholarship, pledging that I wanted our campus to be one of integrity, known for democratic principles. I applauded and supported Phi Theta Kappa, a national junior college honors society, often addressing its state and regional conventions. Once I drove over ice from Snyder to San Antonio to address this group, covering the some 250 miles in 12 hours—yes, that's about 20 MPH—and I arrived just in time to shave before my 10 a.m. assembly. That was at a period in my life when I thought I HAD to be some place. Looking back, I feel less guilty about accepting the group's honorary lifetime membership....

Brenda and I wanted to be encouragers. We frequently had students in our home, and regularly invited student leaders to express their concerns to me. A full two years had passed before I asked the student body president if there was ANYTHING I could do to make life better for WTC students. He slowly responded, "Yes, I think they'd all like it if we could have a cold drink machine in the dormitory." Boy, that was an easy one! I didn't have to gaze toward the horizon, take the matter under advisement or plug it into the equation—we got the kids a cold drink machine. (Over the years, I have found students to be overwhelmingly understanding, cooperative and helpful—with very few exceptions....)

During most weekends, the WTC dormitory became a ghost town. Most of the students had automobiles—or pick-ups (one was awfully proud of his 1968 Lincoln Continental Mark IV truck)—and they headed home for Momma's cooking and clean laundry. Left in the dorm were basketball players, most of whom were from out of state and most of whom had no transportation. Since it was not feasible to keep the cafeteria open after lunch on Fridays, we gave the basketballers a stipend—I think it was $15 each—for weekend meals. The team captain was permitted to drive the WTC bus to various eating places....

Brenda just couldn't stand this arrangement of their having to eat out so often and came up with a plan that worked every Sunday evening during our years in Snyder. Every week, she would prepare home-made dishes, augmenting them with fried chicken or barbecue brought in. Sometimes, she even prepared a big roast, and we served the food to the team in our home or in the student center. Though a ton of work for her, the players loved the arrangement, and our family spent many pleasant hours with them....

◆ ◆ ◆

THESE GUYS, MOSTLY from northern and eastern cities, were wide-eyed at the expanses of West Texas and its vast oil fields. One weekend, they were guests at the Diamond M Ranch, where the owners, Bill and Evelyn Davies, prepared a barbecue dinner.

After dinner, we loaded the guys on the back of pickup trucks and drove around the ranch. We had been driving several minutes when I asked them if they could imagine one family owning such a large ranch. "You mean one family owns this?" a New Yorker responded, "I am shocked. I thought this was like a national park—just like, well maybe, just OUT HERE!"

◆ ◆ ◆

A primary ongoing effort, both at WTC and earlier at Tarrant County, was to legitimatize two-year colleges. For several decades, dating back to the early years of the century, two-year schools generally were looked upon as being "second class," or places of last resort. In some cases, that was correct. For several decades, fewer than 10 percent of American college students were in these schools. By the mid-1970's, the situation had dramatically changed. Two-year schools became far more comprehensive and integral parts of the communities they served. By the 1970's, some 60 percent of the nation's freshman and sophomore students were in two-year institutions. With the junior colleges' new status, heightened respect soon followed. Senior institutions, realizing that much of their success depended on recruiting graduates of these schools, became far more lenient and cooperative relative to transfer of credits.

Whenever I saw our graduates who had transferred to senior institutions, I always asked if there had been any problems with transfer of credits. Almost always, the answer was "no." One girl answered affirmatively, and I was shaken when she said she lost 13 credit hours in transfer. "My, that's a semester's work; is it possible you took the wrong courses?" I asked.... "No, I made the wrong grades," she admitted....

◆ ◆ ◆

Chapter Seven

Forgiven and Freedom to Forgive

Lessons in forgiveness are often provided by unlikely people and unexpected situations. Three stand out—two from beloved student friends, and the other from a personal experience in high school.

It was an exciting prospect, back in 1954, for kids in rural Early High School to learn that the very next year, a band director would be employed to organize the school's first-ever band. During the school's first quarter-century, the closest we got to instrumental music was piano accompaniment for the choir, and drums—one bass and a couple of snares—which were largely heard at football games above the screams of the pep squad and cheerleaders.

Most of the 30 or so aspirants in grades seven through 12 who signed up for band didn't know a sharp from a flat, and any exposure to music was limited to singing in the shower or playing the radio. A smattering had limited piano or guitar instruction; needless to say, I was in the former group....

In the summer, kids signing up for band were caught up in wide-eyed anticipation of what the director might be like. It would almost certainly be a man in those days. Would he be young or old? Shy or outgoing? Disciplined or easy-going? Perhaps more pertinent would have been the question of whether he would be a level-headed person….

When August rolled around, the director called a meeting. He was gentle, bald, old (we thought toward 70, but maybe just 65) and was he ever level-headed! Before long, we were referring to him as the most level-headed man in Brown County. He was a snuff dipper, you see, and snuff juice rolled out of each corner of his mouth at exactly the same rate; that's about as level as it gets!

A band director all of his adult life, he took pride in being able to play all the instruments, and we learned, early on, how critical it was to hit the right notes on the first try. When we didn't, he grabbed the instrument to "show us how." He never wiped off the mouth pieces; he just cut loose playing. Then, he would hand the horn back to us with a strong admonition: "Now you do it." Since he didn't wipe off the mouth pieces, we didn't dare do so, either—never mind some snuff juice made its way to the very spot where our lips met the horn. As I said, we tried really hard to avoid this situation, which was viewed as yucky by most of us, but beyond hilarious for the percussion section….(Snuff juice hardly ever went from his hands to the drumsticks, but if it did, it didn't seem nearly as bad just to get the stuff on your hand.)

◆ ◆ ◆

FRIDAY NIGHTS, PARTICULARLY in the 1950's, were big in Texas for a single reason: high school football. This was particularly true in small towns (which ours was) and in West Texas (where we were).

Digression aside, football season opened at Gorman, Texas, where we were to sport our new uniforms, play the simplest of marches called "Our Director," and present one marching formation that, at the time, seemed fairly intricate for us. With some 25 kids suited out for the marching band, we were to spell the word "Hi" as the highlight of our half-time show. (Hey now, remember we were the greenest of musicians, busy trying to stay in fairly straight lines, read the music perched on our instruments and blow at the right time....)

An additional complication was learning how to put on the band uniform. I had heard of junior high school athletes having to be coached as to which pad goes where, but didn't dream it would apply to band uniforms, too. They arrived the day of the game, so we had to be quick studies of just how to do the laces, which brass buttons to fasten, how to attach the foot-long feather plume into the foot-tall headpieces and how to get the braids in place over the left shoulder. (The braids, I should add, were of the devil; explanation later....) We were off on an hour-long bus ride to Gorman, me thinking of the one flat I had to negotiate on my baritone horn in "Our Director." I got my uniform on with minimal difficulty, but the braid seemed to be extremely long, drooping limply from my shoulder down past my waist....

Before we knew it, the first half ended. We took the field, marching its length before a counter-march back to mid-field, where "Hi" would be formed. As I made the sharp turn near the end zone, the long braid flopped out, lassoing Linda Smith's clarinet. It was lodged under a key, and while the rest proceeded back toward mid-field, she and I were frantically trying to get my braid from her clarinet. Linda—clearly the victim—told me later that she understood why I felt like I had to jerk the braid free without regard to damage to the clarinet. After all, she was simply a part of the "H"; they could make do. I, however, had to dot the "i." I ran at full throttle, arriving there just in time to dot the letter. (From that time until this, my eye still twitches when someone mentions "dotting every 'i.'")

What humiliation! I didn't think I could face my parents, the band director or fellow students—ever again. I had heard of the sixth grader who spent 30 minutes trying unsuccessfully trying to do math homework; he finally declared, "I wish I had this homework done, was married and dead!" I felt just that way. Life was over....

But it wasn't! I was the object of forgiveness—to a person. Our band director, wiping snuff juice away, assured me that it could have happened to anybody, and in just a few minutes, he had repaired Linda's clarinet. My folks said they had never seen an "i" better dotted. Sunrise, promised the following morning, occurred. But, the marching incident—for all people except me—ignited riotous laughter from that night on....I think I broke into my first smile a couple of years later at graduation.

Who would have thought a youngster could feel so forgiven by so many for what seemed at the time to be such a grievous blunder? My faith was restored, and I was a participant in an experience that has helped me, across the years, to decide what to laugh at, and when to laugh at it.

◆ ◆ ◆

More than 30 years later, Charles Chapman, a college freshman from San Antonio, showed hundreds of students and employees of Howard Payne University an ultimate act of forgiveness. Only a few weeks after fall classes began, Charles got a call from home that his mother had been murdered. Imagine our shock to learn that not only had she been murdered, the act was committed by one of Charles' high school friends. The killer perhaps didn't have murder on his mind when he broke open the door to the Chapman home that day, but he did have a gun. He had no idea anyone was at home, and when Mrs. Chapman entered the room behind him, he turned and fired, killing her instantly.

When Charles returned to campus, he was enveloped in love—from fellow students, teachers, counselors and others. In fact, it was rare to seem him on campus that he wasn't huddled with others, no doubt regaining a sense of normalcy with each passing day....

A few days later, Charles told me he would like to "say a few words" during chapel services. Sometimes, such requests were suspect, made by students unprepared for their next class. Their logic, quite simply, was that if they could filibuster long enough, the next class period would be shortened, and a dreaded test would have to be postponed for another day....

But this was not a typical request and Charles was not a typical student. I introduced him, and he walked slowly to the lectern, steadying himself by gripping it with both hands. He thanked those who had helped him cope, citing numerous people who had been particularly helpful. "You helped me tie knots in my thread of life, and without these knots, I'm sure I would have slipped off," he said, "Thank you." Then, he dropped the bombshell no one expected....

"More important than my thanking you, though, is to let you know that I have forgiven my friend." He spoke the words slowly, his eyes sweeping the audience. There was no doubt but that his sentiment was heart-felt, studied and cried out to be shared....

The audience was stunned. Usually by this time, students were restless, eager to get out of chapel, even if not eager to get to class. It was totally quiet. Wheels were turning in many heads, I am sure, as each of us thought of insignificant acts that we had not forgiven. Yet, here was an 18-year-old man who, in a brief statement, made all of us rethink the importance of forgiveness.

Word got out to churches, as well as to groups in our community, about the young man who forgave the friend who killed his mother. He was invited to speak, recounting his personal experience again and again. It was a lesson always timely, and always important....

TOWARD SEMESTER'S END, I realized late on a Friday afternoon that the day's mail had not yet been opened. I flipped through it, discarding the third class stuff, and sat up in my chair when I saw scrawled on the front of an envelope, "Personal and Confidential." (I have learned, over the years, that such envelopes rarely contain letters from people telling you what a great job you are doing.) I opened it quickly, fearing the worst, even more so when I glanced to see who signed it. "Anonymous." Oh boy! If "Personal and Confidential" are bad, throw in "Anonymous," and you can really feel the headache coming on.

But wait. The letter began, "Dear Mr. President: Because of Charles Chapman, I have decided not to commit suicide...." The writer went on to say that suicide had been a central thought until hearing Chapman's recent testimony. The writer explained that following his remarks, life seemed more manageable.... In a matter of minutes, suicide seemed very wrong and living seemed very right....The writer suggested that an award was very much in order for Charles—but that it would mean more if it were presented by the college. (I keep mentioning "the writer" because I don't know if it was a man or woman, student or non-student, resident or visitor, old or young, democrat or republican, etc.)

My head cleared as I thought back over the previous couple of minutes. Instead of a dreaded letter, this was one of thanksgiving. Did it matter that it was signed "Anonymous"? Of course not! Tears coursed down my face, and I fumbled to find a file folder. This letter must be retained. I filed the letter away, then went out into the hall for a drink of water.

It was late in the day, and administration building staff was exiting for the weekend. I looked down the hallway, noticing one student, seemingly just standing there. I trembled when I realized the student was Charles Chapman. I asked him to come into my office, because I had just read a letter about him. He didn't realize, of course, that his presence—in that moment, at that place, at the very time I was reading the letter—seemed to me to be a divine appointment of God—one of invigoration, assurance and comfort.

I handed him the letter. As he read it, we both cried. Before he left, I told him that it was late in the budget year, and that the college wouldn't be able to afford a special award for him. I went from tears to a small chuckle, knowing that this matter's importance far exceeded mere awards. Again, Charles said just the right thing, "I don't need your award; I have His reward," he smiled, his finger pointing toward the heavens....

Four years later, at graduation, when I handed him his diploma, I whispered, "Charles, thank you...for teaching us...."

◆ ◆ ◆

We knew them both well, this couple so in love during our closing years at Howard Payne. Kathy Jo Muirhead, a lovely co-ed from Eastland, smiled her way into our hearts and the hearts of hundreds of others across the campus. A marvelous Christian revered by students and faculty alike, she was there to train to become a school teacher. (Howard Payne, for more than a century, has been known as an institution with a caring faculty, and is highly regarded for teacher-training and minister-training programs.)

We had one of each in Kathy Jo and Shawn Brown in these two popular disciplines; a majority of the student body chooses these majors. She and Shawn both were active in the Baptist Student Ministry, and it was through this campus organization that they became friends....

During her final years at Howard Payne and pre-marriage years following graduation, Kathy Jo shared housing with two of our daughters, Jana and Jeanie. She was—and is—in so many ways, part of our family. After Kathy Jo and Shawn started dating, both of them were in our home often. Brenda put more water in the soup....

That last year of college, Kathy Jo wasn't often seen without her suitor! Shawn, a student from San Angelo, came to Howard Payne to study church youth ministry and pitch for the baseball team. He dropped out of baseball after one season; he simply ran out of time. In addition to full-time study, he was busy with part-time youth ministry at an out-of-town church and then, well, Kathy Jo came into his picture....

◆ ◆ ◆

Who knows if it was really love at first sight? Well, they knew—and the rest of us could tell—that it was the real deal. Jana and Jeanie were participants in their Eastland, Texas, wedding that was held in her home church on a December day in 1997. It was a grand occasion, memorable for many reasons. There were live doves in a cage near the altar, and Christmas decorations adorning First Baptist Church added beauty to the ceremony. Kathy Jo's parents—as well as the rest of us—beamed at her beauty and the joy and the commitment the young couple held for God and for each other. Unfortunately, there was no parental joy for Shawn. His mother had died during his sophomore year of high school, and his dad had moved to another state several years before that....

The next fall, they were together in Fort Worth as man and wife. Kathy Jo was teaching school; Shawn was a full-time student at Southwestern Baptist Theological Seminary. They were blissfully happy. Shawn had a part-time job, but still they found time to be together—talking, laughing, sharing, planning....

◆ ◆ ◆

AND THEN, ON a fateful Wednesday night in September of 1999, some 21 months after their marriage, their world caved in. Shawn was already at a youth concert at Wedgwood Baptist Church, where he and Kathy Jo were members and taught a children's Sunday School class. They were there for just about all the services, but this night, Kathy Jo was running a bit behind. She was on a "child-keeping" assignment for a friend after school.

When she arrived, she saw people running from the church, not knowing, of course, that a few minutes before, a crazed gunman had invaded the service, opening fire on the congregation. Some of the people thought it was part of a youth skit. But no, this was as real as it gets. Seven people died, and Shawn was the first man killed; several others were critically injured.

Kathy Jo was restrained from entering the building and didn't know for sure that Shawn was a victim until several hours later. In the meantime, Jana and her husband, Kyle, arrived from Waco; they were there when the terrible news was learned. Shawn had been killed instantly....Less than two years earlier, they had helped her plan her wedding; now, they would help her plan her husband's funeral....There were other memorial services to be held, media responses to field from hundreds of reporters and a plethora of other details, many of them hitting all at once. Within hours, Kathy Jo decided that she simply must make remarks at Shawn's funeral. She prayed for the strength and composure to do so, and for just the right words. It was a blessed time; her prayers were clearly answered. She found just the right words, claiming God's promise that we "are never left comfortless," and pressed on to the next hours, days and months, sustained by her prayers—and the prayers of others. (At the funeral, she finally met Shawn's dad....)

We, and hundreds of others, have marveled at Kathy Jo's forgiving spirit. Though devastated and sometimes mired in the valley of despair, she has persevered—yes, she has even forgiven the man who killed her husband! She has shared her gripping testimony at numerous churches and spoken for women's groups all over Texas. She is truly remarkable. Brenda and I were with her on the first anniversary of the tragedy.

There were many tears as we watched the premiere showing of a touching video tribute to the victims of the Wedgwood tragedy by media personnel at the North

American Mission Board. (Later, it was seen on national television.) We heard, yet again, those words from Kathy Jo's lips: "If we had just known the man was sick, we would have invited him to our home. Shawn would have counseled him while I cooked supper for him." (Kathy Jo is now Mrs. Marc Rogers; her husband is a Methodist minister. They reside in Fort Worth, Texas.)

◆ ◆ ◆

WHAT A TESTIMONY she is in this matter of forgiveness! She musters her courage and forges on, because she chooses to do so. We can all make similar decisions to forgive, even when we are most hurt, and to accept the hands of our friends when we don't know what else to do. Finally, in our march toward tomorrow, we must always cling to the mustard seed of faith within us that has sustained many through the darkest hours....

◆ ◆ ◆

Chapter Eight

Howard Payne Early, Howard Payne Late

When it became known in 1985 that there would be a new president at Howard Payne, I was contacted by an alumnus, Dr. Gene Porter. A respected Brownwood businessman who had served for many years on the Board of Trustees, he made it clear that his query was made independent of other members of the presidential search committee. I was granted what might be called a courtesy interview; it was cordial enough, but clear to me early on that a majority of the committee didn't view me as a top candidate for the presidency. I returned to Snyder, feeling that the HPU presidency would go to another candidate....But, Dr. Porter urged me to "hold on" and to be patient....

◆ ◆ ◆

Qualifications aside, I was in a position to view HPU from many perspectives. As a lad growing up in Brown County, it was the first name of a higher education institution I ever heard. During junior high and high school, I attended football and basketball games played by the Yellow Jackets. I held an HPU degree (with triple majors), had been on the full-time staff for two years, and had been a member of the university's Board of Trustees for eight years. As a member of that Board, I had voted to hire my predecessor six years earlier. I had been cited as "Alumnus of the Year," riding with my family in a homecoming parade convertible. Yes, I felt I knew the school pretty well, and just might be able to rally the alumni to help rescue a school that was on "life support." Enrollment had dwindled from a high of some 1,500 to about 700, and the morale was at low ebb....

I Love a Parade...
Over the years, there were numerous kinds of conveyances for homecoming parades. Brenda and I have ridden in convertibles, wagons and on top of floats. Here, I'm atop a float. (I balked at the offer to ride a horse in any parades.)

As Dr. Porter instructed, I remained patient, even staying through the noon hour at my office on the day the Board met to name a new president. A valued Snyder friend, Jimmie Joe Key, who had flown me in his plane to several speaking engagements, was ready to whisk me to Brownwood, if needed. It was almost 12:30, but the phone remained silent. Suddenly, it occurred to me that the Western Texas College switchboard was closed from noon until 1 p.m. So, I situated myself in front of the switchboard, praying that if a call came in, I would have sense enough answer it correctly! It rang a couple of times, and I played the part of PBX operator, answering "Western Texas College"; in both cases, the parties opted to call back later, but just before 1 p.m., the call I was hoping for came....

On the other end was Dr. Leon Aduddell, HPU Trustee President. He informed me that I had just been hired (pending my acceptance) on a majority vote of the Board, and that I should come to Brownwood ASAP. We had a tail wind, arriving in Brownwood in well under an hour. I was greeted there by a very divided Board. I learned later that the presidential search committee had proposed another name for the presidency, but the Board vote failed. Then, Dr. Porter, his minority report in hand and words rehearsed, presented my name. Then came the critical vote; I was elected, 16-14. (Happily, I enjoyed strong Board support within a matter of months.)

◆ ◆ ◆

Brenda and I had already decided that if the Board voted favorably—no matter how close the vote—we would accept the challenge. Financially, it was a lateral move. The salary was in the mid-$50's, plus housing and an automobile. Knowing then—and now—that the faculty and staff at HPU have historically served there sacrificially, I viewed the compensation as fair. I made it clear, though, that I thought the president's home—then located several miles from the campus—should be on or near the campus. The Board agreed to sell the home and purchase another.

Within a few weeks, we ended our work at WTC, turned in our keys and made the move to Brownwood. Not long after we got there, I got an "overdue" reminder from the WTC librarian. It seems that I had checked out a book that should have been turned in weeks earlier. Finally, I remembered. R. C. Patton, our Board of Trustees chairman, knew I had the book, and asked if I would let him read it when I finished. That's what I did, reporting same to the librarian. I never did hear if the chairman had to pay the late fee....

Oh, you want to know the name of the over-due book? It was a biography of a great West Texan, Congressman George Mahon, *An Honest Man.*

◆ ◆ ◆

Our first home in Brownwood was rented. It was an historic three-story structure built in 1903 by a local physician; it was referred to by his name, "The Rogers Home." It was at 707 Center Avenue, adjacent to what two years later would become the president's home at 701 Center. Mr. and Mrs. Charles Lockwood, owners of the property for many years, opted for a smaller home when their children were grown. They were gracious to rent the home to the school until it sold....

From time to time, we left for a few hours, allowing prospective buyers to tour the magnificent old home. One Saturday morning, we were asked to leave for a couple of hours. We were not inconvenienced—I needed to interview some prospective faculty members, and Brenda was happy to go shopping. The prospective teachers I visited that morning were a husband and wife duo who had recently completed doctorates at Texas Tech. They were shocked by our anemic faculty salaries, so the interview was fairly brief. "Oh, well," the man mentioned, "I guess we ought to go ahead and look at the old house anyway." (Yes, they were looking to buy the very home we were living in, hoping to buy it if they had joined the HPU family....) Thankfully, we still had the same roof over our heads—for the next few months.

◆ ◆ ◆

WITHIN A YEAR of our arrival, the home did sell, and for the next few months, we lived in another rental home a couple of miles from the campus. Behind the scenes, several of our board members were negotiating to purchase the beautiful home at 701 Center. Built in 1901 by the Walker family, it was listed in both State and National historic registries. The Walkers owned a highly successful wholesale grocery business, and spared no expense in building what was, for many years, Brownwood's finest home. It featured rich wood treatment inside, with wraparound porches on the first, second and third floors.

President's Home
Howard Payne president's home at 701 Center Avenue, one block north of the campus. A few visitors thought it to be a funeral home, some thought it was where they could take driver's education and some out-of-town college kids assumed it was a fraternity house.

Initially, the third floor was used as a "ballroom." Many times I've admitted we used it for the same thing—a place for bowling balls, tennis balls, golf balls....(In truth, it became a hang-out for students. A pool table, ping-pong table, stereo and television/VCR were inviting, as was the balcony overlooking 100-year-old pecan and oak trees. Many times, we went to bed at night, asking students lingering on the third floor to exit by the back door and lock it....)

Soon those who loved the university—its faculty, students, alumni and Central Texas friends—were fully engaged in resuscitating a school that had served the state since 1889, and still trumpeted its slogan: "Where everybody is somebody." This has been a core belief as long as I can recall. The value of the individual has been underscored by faculty and others—year after year. HPU, supported by Baptists of Texas, had helped me greatly in developing self-confidence during formative student years, and I was convinced that a liberal arts institution, couched in Christian values, remained sorely needed.

They had a big dinner to welcome our family. About a thousand guests broke bread at Brownwood Coliseum, and another 500 showed up for the festivities following the meal. It was a joyous time, complete with organ music. Brenda and I cringed a bit when the organist broke into "Happy Times are Here Again." (My predecessor was seated at the next table....) The emcee introduced me as a "former United Methodist" coming back to Howard Payne. I corrected him, explaining that "I was a Methodist before they were United, and joined the Baptists because I thought they were!"

J. R. Beadel, whose family has been extremely generous to the school, walked to the microphone, announcing a gift of $25,000. I accepted his check, thinking that maybe fund-raising wouldn't be such a task after all. (I was wrong, and Dr. Guy D. Newman, HPU's president from 1955-72 and a man I designated as Chancellor soon after arrival, was right. He had told me about a scriptural reference he wanted on his gravestone—"And it came to pass the beggar died!" In retrospect, that might be an appropriate epitaph for the president of any church-supported college.)

◆ ◆ ◆

There was so much we didn't have. Most facilities were old and needed repair. Some dormitories were not air-conditioned, and the phone system was, well, primitive! There was one phone in the hall of each dormitory wing—each serving a couple of dozen students. Perhaps one reason that most students got along well is that if one didn't, he or she likely didn't get yelled at when phone calls came in! (Within five years, there was a new system in place with phone and Internet access in every room....)

Yes, there was an immense sense of "want to" among all who loved the school. I talked about the importance of freshmen, friends and funds, and the work began. We all made hundreds of phone calls; other contacts were made, and soon, the battle turned....In short, it was a story of working the highways and the side roads. It reminded me of a sign posted at Hugh White's Highland Café and Grocery in Alpine. It read (excuse the grammar): "There ain't hardly any business got these days that ain't went out after!"

◆ ◆ ◆

STUDENTS KIDDED THAT they came to Howard Payne "on purpose." Of Texas' eight Baptist universities, it is the only one not located on an interstate highway, and there are no significant population pockets within 100 miles. And, where there was substantial population, other institutions already existed. They made their own fun, as they say, inventing Jacket Golf, which involved golf clubs whacking tennis balls toward various objects on campus. They also flocked to Lake Brownwood for swimming and water sports. On many beautiful nights, carloads of students made the 20-mile drive to the old suspension bridge spanning the Colorado River for—whatever.

At the time, there was one four-screen movie theatre located in a very modest mall (kids sometimes called it the "hall.") One weekend, the students offered a "dorm-in" movie. Unlike the frequent Friday night movies offered in the auditorium, this one was outdoors. They stitched together several bed sheets, draping them from the fourth floor of Veda Hodge Dormitory, the residence hall for women. Across the street from the fourth floor of Jennings Hall, a men's facility, the projector was aimed straight at the bedsheet screen, and it was a direct hit!

Students brought yard chairs, blankets and even sofas—and some watched the movie from the backs of pick-up trucks—in what became a magical evening. Brenda and I loved seeing them having fun in this unique way. We walked among them, laughing, chatting and handing out popcorn....

◆ ◆ ◆

THE STUDENTS' FIRST dose of ingenuity was noticed when I was introduced on campus as being born "near May." Several said, "Now let's get more specific—were you born in late April or early June?" Classmate Bill Stovall, a decorated sports editor at the BROWNWOOD BULLETIN for some 40 years loved it. In numerous columns, he loved to work in a reference to my humble origin....

Concerning ingenuity, the term is a perfect fit for Michael Stanard. He had the "look" folks who've never been to Texas imagine Texans look like. With a slow drawl and disarming smile, Mike also "talked Texas." He was rarely seen without his cowboy hat that had an over-sized turkey feather stuck in the brim. Mike seemed to be the source for whatever one might want to buy—and he could get it for you wholesale!

Early on, Brenda and I were urged to see his room in the dormitory, and to help find a violation; other authorities couldn't! When we visited it, we could hardly believe what we saw. Mike had constructed a log cabin (actually two tiny rooms) without driving a single nail into the dorm walls, or violating in any way our housing rules. There was primitive furniture, and the place looked for all the world like where Davy Crockett might hang out. He had broken no rules; in fact, I complimented his creative genius. We often showed prospective students and their parents what could be done with a dorm room!

Stanard likewise was well-known for donning the "stinger disguise" as the Yellow Jacket mascot at athletic events. Once he rode his bicycle—in full disguise—for the entire 80-mile trip for a basketball game in Abilene. During his senior year, he married Linda Rich, a pretty co-ed, in a wedding ceremony conducted on Center Avenue—the street running between the dormitories. Traffic was rerouted for a few minutes as the knot was tied. (For the ceremony, Michael took off his hat....)

◆ ◆ ◆

During the almost 12 years of my presidency, we lost just one student. We have estimated that during this tenure, HPU students—most of whom had automobiles—drove well in excess of 100 million miles. There were some accidents and a few injuries, but not one fatality. This statistic boggles my mind. The one loss—unrelated to automobile accidents—stung deeply. His name was Chris Green....

During his junior year in high school, Chris was diagnosed with lupus. The disease limited his activities, but the doctors explained that while it typically is terminal, many victims live with the disease for many years. They suggested that he get on with life....When his parents, Mr. and Mrs. Malvin Green of Shiner, brought him to campus, they were concerned that his periodic medical treatment would be 80 miles away, in Abilene. Chris didn't have a car, and Mr. Green asked if some arrangements could be made for his son. I assured him that this would be no problem....

I figured student groups would be happy to accommodate Chris. It turned out that this was not necessary. Telling the story that night, I was in no way surprised by Brenda's response. "I'll take him," she said, warning me that she wanted no credit or fanfare for so doing. During the next several months, she drove him to Abilene (80 miles away) several times. In each case, there would be lab work, and sometimes a lengthy doctor's visit. Each trip required almost a full day, and soon, Chris was a regular visitor in our home. He and Brenda would laugh about something that happened on the most recent medical trip, or where they had lunch....

He was a shy young man, eager to be accepted by campus groups. Chris was, of course, accommodated. Upon entering the cafeteria, members of a fraternity he was later to join, would greet him with a chorus, "There's Chris Green—let's give Chris Green a hand." Chris would move down the food line, red-faced, as the diners provided a rousing cheer. As the semester wore on and his confidence grew, he made his own cafeteria announcement: "Here's Chris Green. Let's give Chris Green a hand!" He would applaud himself, then endure the hisses his announcement would inevitably evoke. From day one, other students saw in him a genuine Christian spirit and maturity beyond his years.

◆ ◆ ◆

None of us was ready for the jolting news toward the end of Chris' freshman year. He had experienced a seizure, and was transferred from the Brownwood hospital to another one in Abilene. Doctors rightly said that he had no medical chance for survival. Within hours, he was gone. His parents, people of faith and courage, then made the drive back to Brownwood to collect Chris' belongings from his dorm room. Brenda and I helped them, as did dorm director Mike Kennamer. We quietly wept as the truck was loaded. Two days later, we and more than 100 HPU students were in Shiner, some 250 miles away, for the memorial service for a youngster who had "given a hand as he accepted a hand." To their credit, the Greens have continued to have positive feelings toward Howard Payne. In fact, their daughter, Erin, is now a graduate, and their other son, Brent, is an HPU senior....

◆ ◆ ◆

During my presidency, only two students received the President's Award, presented at graduation. The first was

Susan Hester. Her husband, Dennis, also an HPU graduate, is now a Baptist minister. They were married near the mid-point of their college years, and during their senior year, their daughter, Katy, was born. Unfortunately, she was born with so many physical impairments, little hope was offered for her survival. She wound up at a hospital in the Metroplex, and, slowly and painfully, made strides to the degree that survival was no longer an issue. Still, she would require numerous surgeries over the coming years. Through it all, Susan remained in school, graduating summa cum laude with a perfect 4.0 grade point average for the four years.

4.0 and More...
Susan Hester was one of two graduates to receive the President's Award during our almost 12 years in the presidency. She had a 4.0 gradepoint average, and was a champion in every respect. (The other person to receive this honor was David Cozart.)

The other designee was David Cozart. He arrived at HPU from Snyder, Texas, where he had been Student Body President and was the recipient of numerous other honors. He continued to distinguish himself at HPU, where he made exemplary grades and was elected Student Body President. From the day he arrived on campus, he seemed intent not merely to learn facts, but also how to serve. It was common to see him in faculty offices, always probing the minds of others who had been further down the trail. He married Lori Etchison, also an HPU graduate, and soon they were in Waco, Texas. They both took jobs and he enrolled at Truett Seminary of Baylor University.

All seemed well, but all was not well. David was diagnosed with testicular cancer, and surgery was required. (Perhaps the only good news at the time was that David's folks had insisted that he have interim medical coverage for the brief time he would be uninsured prior to beginning his new job.)

Thankfully, the surgery was successful, but radiation and continued treatment were ordered. He was warned that his hair would fall out as a result of radiation…. Some of his friends thought a celebration was in order and asked if I could come to Waco to make some remarks at the party. I already had a speaking engagement out of town and was unable to accept. They understood, but asked if I would send remarks via video tape; David's friends had decided to wear toboggans at the event honoring him, so they asked me to wear one on the video tape. Of course I would….I donned the cap, made sure the videographer got some close-ups, and sent it to the party planners….

No one told me that the party had to be delayed. In fact, several months passed, and by this time, David's health was back to normal. He was sporting a full head of hair when they had the party, so obviously no one wore toboggans that hot summer day—except for the guy in the video….

◆ ◆ ◆

I could—and likely should—provide dozens and dozens and dozens of accounts of people who "found themselves" at Howard Payne—literally. Perhaps there can be more accounts in another book. Before chapter's end, however, I must reflect on a few more. One is Dr. James McEachern, a classmate. When he arrived at HPU, he didn't think much of himself. Life had tossed him about except for those years spent with his grandparents near Lamesa. His mother was married eight times, and his father, three. He knew much sadness.

During summers at college, he wound up selling books—mostly Bibles—and he encountered other like-minded guys making their way in sales. A few years later, four of them would found the Tom James Company to market men's custom suits. In the last 35 years, each year has exceeded the previous one in sales; there is a team of more than 600 salespersons in the United States, Great Britain, Spain, Japan and The Netherlands. Last year Tom James' revenues surpassed $253 million. McEachern has served as both President and Chief Executive Officer of the organization.

Jim, whose demeanor redefines humility, remains a staunch supporter of HPU, where he is a member of the Board of Trustees. He holds the honorary doctorate from HPU, and has become one of its most generous benefactors. More than once, he has credited me with "showing him the joy of giving." I just wish I had been able to cause many others to experience such joy! (Graduates of the Ovilla Christian School, which he helped found, find that Dr. McEachern pays for 2/3 of their tuition charges if they attend HPU.)

◆ ◆ ◆

TOWARD THE END of my presidency, three young men whose common bond was pre-med training made us very, very proud. They all were admitted to medical schools, all continued to distinguish themselves, and all are currently medical doctors. They are Drs. Jeremy Denning, Tom Collins and Dan Murray.

Jeremy, a Brownwood High School graduate, began college at Southern Methodist University. After his freshman year, he asked if he could live in the "honors apartment" behind our home. Six or seven guys, usually strong academicians and/or students who couldn't or didn't want to live in the dorm, regularly lived there—"to defend my wife and daughters when I'm away," I always maintained. For whatever reason, HPU offered a science course Jeremy needed that was not available at SMU that summer. He liked HPU very much, fretting toward the end of the summer about whether to re-enroll at SMU, or transfer to HPU. I was able to make his choice a tough one. Some local benefactors, learning of his potential, agreed to pay his entire tuition charges if he remained at HPU. "But where would I live?" he questioned, not really interested in living in a dormitory.

Jeanie, our youngest, had just moved to the women's dorm, leaving us with three empty bedrooms in the president's home. Brenda and I agreed that Jeremy could live with us for a few weeks until another place was available....The two weeks became two months and the two months became two years, and there he was, still in the bedroom that had been Jeanie's. In the meantime, he ate meals with us, Brenda did his laundry and he was, for those two years, the son we never had. He was studious and appreciative; there was never a minute's problem. Taking the M-CAT was a common topic of discussion....

He was admitted to the University of Texas Health Science School in Houston, and there his major professor was the colorful Dr. Red Duke, the one frequently seen on television. His major was neurosurgery, and the next year, he was to be joined at the same medical school by Tom Collins...

◆ ◆ ◆

Tom, a high school football star in California, received an appointment to West Point to play football. He was doing fine there—football-wise and otherwise—but he realized that it would be difficult, in that setting, to pursue pre-med. A relative recommended that he look into Howard Payne, where intercollegiate sports are offered on a non-scholarship basis, and classes and labs come first. I recall his visit to the campus on a Saturday in January; we were watching a National Football League play-off game on television. Tom ate lunch with us, remarking, as we watched the game, how much he would like to see the science building. "You will," I assured him, then called Dr. Ruth Ann Murphy, a member of the science faculty, to see if she could provide a tour.

Tom was shocked—first, that she would provide a personal tour of the facilities for him on a Saturday afternoon, and second, that it could be after the game. He was hooked, and became a favorite student at Howard Payne before joining Jeremy in Houston in med school. There, he was elected President of his class....

Born with intestinal masses outside of his body, Tom was fortunate that a skilled surgeon made it possible for him not only to survive, but to live a normal life. Such surgery was extremely rare at the time. From his early years, Tom's goal has been to emulate that surgeon who saved his life in infancy; he's currently working toward the specialty of pediatric surgery in his residency at Gainesville, Florida....

◆ ◆ ◆

THOUGH AMERICAN BORN, Dan Murray spent most of his pre-college years in Toronto, where his father, Dr. Robert Murray, was a longtime member of the faculty of the University of Toronto Medical School. Dan, a dietary and fitness devotee, rode his bicycle from Canada to Texas, covering the 3,400 miles in 36 days, thus averaging almost 100 miles per day. At Howard Payne, he seemed "into" everything—including track and cheerleading. The same day he took the M-CAT in Abilene, he ran a distance race in the conference track meet. (I urged him to forego the race; he wouldn't.) He, like Tom, was in the Douglas MacArthur Academy of Freedom Honors Program.

He was admitted to the Texas A&M University School of Medicine. Upon beginning study there, one of his textbooks was authored by another man named Murray—his father, Dr. Robert Murray. Dan studied family medicine. During medical school, he was admitted to the United States Air Force. He completed his residency in the summer of '02, and became a Flight Surgeon with the Air Force's special forces. Dr./Capt. Murray faces a minimum three-year commitment. Brenda and I were present for his graduation from medical school, as well as from residency. We swelled with pride when he was named "resident of the year" by Scott and White Hospital. We likewise attended the graduation exercises for Denning, and the next year, for both Collins and Murray.

Jeremy, the kid we had seen studying into the wee hours so many nights when he resided with us, continued to be quite the academician in medical school, earning all A's—a distinction achieved by just one other classmate, a 28-year old Chinese graduate of Harvard University. At his graduation, the medical school presented 19 departmental awards. Six of his colleagues won an award each—Jeremy received six....

It was interesting to hear whispers in the audience, "I've heard of Harvard, but where's Howard Payne?" (I so wanted to tell them that it's a place where everybody is somebody....)

Chapter Nine

O Holey Socks

Christmas 2001 will be remembered as the season when airline security people wasted little time moving the spotlight, of all places, to our shoes! (This was probably a happy event in Holland, surely the Dutch welcomed the chance to get out of those wooden shoes....)

The new airport security policy brings to mind all sorts of thoughts going back to grade school years, where a goodly part of our giggling dealt with footwear....

Poorest of students were spotted on school buses. A barometer of "poorness" often centered on tennis shoes, which all guys, and some girls, wore regularly. Guys, wearing them even on the coldest days, were thought to have no other shoes to wear. Worse than this was seeing the sole-side of shoes long worn out, realizing that the cardboard stuck inside to cover the holes kept their feet a bit dryer. Also, grass burr sticks and stone bruises were minimized.

◆ ◆ ◆

Few would have guessed that a half-century later, tennis shoes would again be barometers, but this time, to gauge affluence. The "right" insignias—yea, even the correct inflation level—reveal those who have arrived. These guys may also go about in tennis shoes year-round, even if they have a closet full of shoes at home from which to choose. Tens of millions of Americans, particularly those with memories stretching back as far as mine does, remain self-conscious to this day with nothing to be self-conscious about. And again, we start with the feet!

Who among us has not been embarrassed not only by our shoes, but by our socks? In our early lives, little thought was given to whether socks "matched" pants or shoes, but what surely mattered was whether we wore socks that we might call "right new," or more likely "religious socks." (That's what we called them when they became "holey," but we wore them anyway.) Mothers might try to darn them, but mended socks not only "showed," they also were uncomfortable! Holey socks simply were to be endured, and typically, the mending job didn't hold, and they were "religious socks" once again....

There were some options concerning how to make do. Holes seemed invariably to first appear in the heels, so wearing high-topped tennis shoes would hide the holes. When wearing dress shoes, a common trick was to pull the socks only about 2/3 of the way on, leaving the toe-end material scrunched up in the front, and the tops riding a bit low. Still, the hole was hidden, and that was the main thing.

Dignity—what little we had—was lost on those cold days when we were lined up to go to the gymnasium, knowing that the first order would be to take off our shoes "so we wouldn't scratch the maple floor." (Truth to tell, the old floor had so many scratches on it, I couldn't imagine a few more hurting anything.) We tried to remember, on scheduled gym days, to "wear good socks," but sometimes on inclement days, we were caught with our "religious socks" on. Then, we learned to take off shoes and socks in the same motion to possibly avoid detection of our worn-out socks. The gymnasium became a "holey place" for me, and for lots of other students....

But all memories of feet don't need to be bad. In fact, there were lessons to be learned. We laughed, on buses and at school, about certain students having "B.O." Not until later years did most of us realize that those letters actually stand for words. Ah, but a "rose by any other name would smell as sweet," and "B.O."—whatever the letters stand for—are at opposite end of the aroma/odor scale! The lesson? There are times to laugh, and times to be silent. In those early years, the latter was the best choice....

I have always admired airline passengers, men and women, with enough self-confidence to kick off their shoes upon taking their seats. Earning additional respect are those who spy areas with seats facing and plop their feet up on vacant seats across from them. Chairs with ottomans in front of a crackling fire seem a bit more appealing, but at long day's end on the flight home, it is a little bit of heaven to find facing seats available. It has taken years, but I have finally come to the place where I can comfortably assume such positions while flying, really not caring if others think it gauche, or if I have on holey socks....

One such flight is particularly memorable. Waking from a nap, I proceeded to the lavatory when the "unoccupied" light came on. Not until I stepped back into the aisle did I realize that I had visited the lavatory in my stocking feet. I took notice when a flight attendant expressed disgust that I would enter the facility without shoes. (She may well have been the newest member of the team, with vivid memories of clean-up duty....)

"You mean you went in there in your stocking feet?" she asked. Maybe I didn't have the perfect answer, but I thought of an acceptable one: "I've seen Herb Kelleher do the same thing," not knowing, of course, whether the Southwest Airlines CEO ever went to the lavatory or if he has a private one. He was, I knew, the reigning cut-up among corporate chiefs, and the all-time favorite of Southwest Airlines personnel....

"Well, he's the only other one I can imagine doing such a thing," the young lady quipped, her eyes brightening and smile widening at the thought of her CEO, whose clowning was as well-known as his business acumen.

At trip's end, I thought such an experience worth repeating, so I dashed off a letter to Mr. Kelleher, a man I have long admired and on whose planes I have so often ridden.

Imagine my surprise, just a few days later, to receive a personal response from Mr. Kelleher, whose letter read in part:

> Your recent letter 'made' my day! Welcome to the "shoeless lavatory club"—we are a rare breed...Although we were unable to positively identify the flight attendant with the quick

retort, I am sure she will never
forget you...

There's a lesson there. From time to time, kick off your shoes, take off your socks and wiggle your toes. Forget the condition of your socks, and feel sorry for the uptight folks who are embarrassed about such matters.

◆ ◆ ◆

THANKFULLY, WE'VE RUN across quite a few people who have seemed "down loose" when others were "up tight." Typically, they have been content to make do with what they have, happy with where they are and open to the challenges of whatever life might bring to their doorstep.

A wonderful example of such a person is Ray Hildebrand. He came to Howard Payne on a partial basketball scholarship. Most students at HPU—and I was one of them—didn't have two coins to rub together, and he fit right in. Typically a reserve on the basketball team, Ray was to star in a far different arena—the world of entertainment.

Most of us knew he had a nice voice and loved to sing. Upon entering the gymnasium, we could often hear him plunking on his guitar. The gymnasium? That's right. In order to economize one semester, he lived in the gym, under the bleachers. He had a cot to sleep on, a chair to sit on and lots of places to dress and shower!

One day, he wrote a song called, "Hey Paula." It was a love song with no real-life application—he didn't have a girlfriend named Paula. In fact, Jill Jackson, a local co-ed, and Ray were mere acquaintances. They sang "Hey Paula" on a local radio station, and it was an instant hit. Record producer Bill Smith invited them to Fort Worth for a recording session and "Hey Paula" was released on the LeCam label.

Interviews and public appearances followed in quick order—never mind Ray didn't own a sport coat and his shoes were past the throw-away stage. I loaned him $15 to assist with wardrobe acquisition, and also had the chance to help them with publicity. It turned out they didn't need my help.

A major recording company bought the rights to "Hey Paula," and you probably know the rest. It was embraced by America, standing alone at the top of the pop charts for three straight weeks in 1963, achieving gold record status. They became the nation's sweethearts—even though they never even dated—and they had fictitious names. The couple was on American Bandstand and other national telecasts....

They needed hay-haulers that summer in Oregon, however, so Ray put stardom aside for agricultural chores. Jill continued on her own, one time depending on Dick Clark to sing Ray's part. Truly, Ray was "down loose."

◆ ◆ ◆

AND SO WAS Gordon Wood. This coaching legend, whose record of 396 wins and nine state championships over the span of 43 years placed him in a class of his own for many years, always seemed relaxed and always ready for whatever came next. His longest coaching stint—and a big part of his record—came at his final stop, Brownwood High School. For the last couple of years I lived in Brownwood following college graduation, Coach Wood was a frequent guest on my radio program, and we became life-long friends. I spoke at several of his athletic banquets, and for the past 40 years, we have swapped stories and shared meals together many times. His final season to coach was 1985; my return to Howard Payne, this time as president, was in December of that year....

Though coaching was over, Coach Wood never entertained the thought of retirement. He has busied himself speaking, establishing a museum, writing a couple of books and always—always—looking for ways to help the underdog. And, whenever he's had some time on his hands, he has whipped out "letters to the editor(s)." (His wife, Katharine—a founder of the soup kitchen for hungry people in Brownwood and the Presbyterian Church's Latch-Key program for children—is a lot like Gordon concerning the underdog, but I don't think she writes many letters.)

Upon retirement, Gordon bought Katherine a new car. When she saw it, she said, "That's beautiful, but I'm not going to drive it." Gordon asked why she felt that way, and her answer was quick: " "I could never enjoy driving a car like that as long as there are so many hungry people in Brownwood." He took it back to the dealer for a refund—and got it.

Perhaps he's always been a letter writer, but I do know this: During my years in the presidency at Howard Payne, it was common to see Coach Wood walking pertly toward the Administration Building, with a sheaf of paper in hand. Invariably, he proposed a "letter to the editor" of one or more area newspapers, and he always had a few thoughts scribbled down. "Maybe you could help me with the final version" was a typical request.

◆ ◆ ◆

Of course I would! This was Gordon Wood, and I assisted with pleasure if I could help him with letter construction. Whatever I was doing was put on hold until the letter or letters were finished. (Immediately, I switched from being a president to a stenographer, and, even though a couple of hours away now, sometimes help by phone and mail.)

Once, while working on a long letter he proposed to send to the TEXAS COACH magazine, it was apparent that the letter might consist of several pages. I wasn't sure what the magazine's limitation might be on length of letters submitted for publication, but the editor's answer when I called was not unanticipated: "For Gordon Wood, it can be as long as he chooses." He's another guy who has determined to stay "down loose" in an "up tight" world, never caught up in self-importance, and committed to a lifetime of championing the underdog! He doesn't drive a new car, either. And, when he grabs a pair of socks that happen to have holes in them, he might—or might not—opt for another pair. If he's got them at least halfway on, he'll likely wear them until day's end....

◆ ◆ ◆

Chapter Ten

Seeing Beyond the Darkness

I OFTEN THINK of dozens of college students who overcame great obstacles in their pilgrimages to college graduation. None stands out, though, quite like Lizzie Phillips, whom I've often accused of "invading" the Howard Payne University campus.

"My name is Lizzie Phillips; I've come to look at the campus; I'm four feet five inches tall, and I'm not a dwarf." She seemed intent on getting all these thoughts on record in the early moments of that first visit in the fall of 1997.

"Let the records show that you are not a dwarf, Lizzie," I responded, knowing that she was stretching it in saying she was "looking" at the campus. I had heard her sing at a Christmas banquet the previous year, and knew she was totally blind....However, she did have limited eyesight in her pre-school years. I also knew she was born with numerous genetic disorders, and had kept life "sunny side up" despite a lifetime of ailments—severe orthopedic problems, painful nerve disorders, and more than two dozen surgeries, some of them life-threatening.

◆ ◆ ◆

WHAT I LEARNED about Lizzie during the next few hours would inspire the most entrenched cynic, and make the world's most incurable optimists sport even wider smiles. Ever nurtured by her loving parents, Gary and Rhonda Phillips, her brother, Greg, and countless other relatives and friends, Lizzie has more often been the encourager rather than the "encouragee."

At Cedar Hill High School, where she received her high school diploma in 1998, she ranked in the top 10% of her class, won state solo and ensemble awards in the a cappella choir and was a leader in the Spanish Honor Society. She was also active in her youth group at First Baptist Church, Duncanville. Her vocal talents are well-known across the state; music has been her constant companion since age five. In those early years, she spent hours and hours with her jam box, singing away. The jam box gave way to taped accompaniments, and Lizzie has been silenced just once—when jaw surgery made it impossible for her to sing for eight long months—months she described as being "just awful."

As the visit that day continued, I mentioned to Lizzie that the afternoon included plans to take some students parasailing at Lake Brownwood. "Oh, I love boats," she responded, and yes, she and her folks would love to come along. It was a Kodak kind of afternoon, and soon we were at the lake on the 32-foot boat, deck hands at the ready to "catch the wind" to inflate the parasail. A dozen or so students also were on board, very much ready to go aloft—some 600 feet above the lake, dangling from the parasail.

Lizzie was co-pilot that afternoon, sitting across from me, her legs barely extending past the seat cushion. As we skimmed across the water, laughter and lively conversation abounded. The topic got around to music, and several contemporary Christian favorites were mentioned. Some students liked Stephen Curtis Chapman best; others chose Point of Grace. One in the back of the boat favored Chicago. "I like Chicago, too," Lizzie said, "But I wasn't sure it was okay to like Chicago." I decided to bluff. "Lizzie, there's nothing wrong with liking Chicago," I assured her, not having a clue about the music of Chicago. I didn't know Chicago from Peoria….

One by one, the students were strapped into the harness, taking off from the back deck. After a few minutes aloft, I hit the button to start bringing flyers back in, but most of them first wanted to be "dunked" before returning to the boat. Dunking usually was easy to do. I would slow the motor, allowing the chute to glide lazily toward the water. I would try to let the flyers get about waist-deep in the water, then accelerate to return them to the air once again. (Sometimes I would miss it four or five feet, but no harm done….)

◆ ◆ ◆

I wondered what I would do if Lizzie wanted to parasail. Soon, she broached the subject. "I would love to parasail, but I can't," Lizzie said. "But my mother can," she added hastily.

In an instant, I contrasted Mrs. Phillips' appearance—upon her hearing the chilling suggestion—with my remembrance of how she boarded the vessel a few minutes earlier. She was cheery, light-hearted and laughing. In an instant, she had become ashen, stiff and resolved. Without hesitation, she said, "Strap me in the harness."

As she prepared for flight, I thought of hundreds of times when I keenly realized parents would do any reasonable thing for their kids. Here, it seemed to me, was a parent jumping to the front of the list, willing to do something clearly in the unreasonable category!

Up she went, the length of two football fields above the lake. Lizzie was laughing heartily, clapping her hands, insistent on a detailed description of her mother's ride. She wanted to know how her mother was doing, how the rope was doing, the boat doing, the sail doing, how I was doing.... "Lizzie, everything is fine," I assured. "That's what I figured," she answered. After a short pause, she commanded, "Dunk her!"

"Dare I dunk Lizzie's mother?" I asked myself. "Of course I would," I decided. I was trying to recruit Lizzie, not her mother, so Rhonda Phillips was dunked before we brought her back on the boat.

Safely back on the boat platform, her cheerful spirit returned. She was now the member of a fairly exclusive group. Not too many people have parasailed on the small lake—one that has far more fishermen than flyers. And Lizzie experienced flight that afternoon, vicariously through her mom....

◆ ◆ ◆

AND WHAT ABOUT Lizzie in 2002? She is a senior at HPU, where her vocal talents have been lauded in many ways, and where her spirit and dogged determination have inspired students and faculty.

An Inspiration For All
Lizzie Phillips, though blind, has as much vision as any person I've ever known. She's a wonderful friend, and has more determination than any person whose path I have crossed. She is a candidate for graduation in December 2002. We should all strive to emulate her.

She walks around campus when she can, and students rally around to push her wheelchair on days when walking is not an option. She has had multiple knee surgeries since starting to college, all aimed at making it possible for her to have a guide dog. When the first one was unsuccessful, she didn't lament, but said, "That dog will just have to learn to get along without me."

At this writing, she has two goals, both near at hand and sharp in focus. College graduation awaits in December, and the very next month, she's to be in Florida to meet her guide dog, and undergo training for that new chapter in her life....

Lizzie's life and philosophy have shown many people that they are capable of facing whatever comes next. Though her eyesight is dark, Lizzie finds the light in her life through constant optimism, unyielding faith and a vision for the future all of us should hope to have....

◆ ◆ ◆

Chapter Eleven

Tassel Tales—Endings or Beginnings?

Graduation is a very big deal. Parents insist on it, whether the graduation is marking completion of preschool, kindergarten, elementary school, high school, college or professional school. All have heard, time and again, "My kids are going to have 'it' better than I did." And "it" includes graduation exercises. In Texas, we pretty much use "graduation" and "commencement" interchangeably. I guess it depends on whether we are looking backward or forward at the ceremonies. For the honorees, I believe most high school graduates are "thinking backward," and figure what they've accomplished is reason for celebration, receiving gifts and collecting honors. They can "look forward" later at college commencement....

From my standpoint, consideration will be limited to high school and college events, mostly those where I have spoken and/or presided. Perhaps the most important lesson I've learned as a participant is this: It is virtually impossible to make ceremonies too short! Prospective graduates have counted the days to the event, but then, once assembled, they soon reach the fidgety stage, eager to receive the coveted diplomas, turn their tassels and then get the heck out for a night of merry-making.

◆ ◆ ◆

SPEAKERS OFTEN JOKE about graduates remembering little or nothing of what they say even as recently as a year after commencement. Those who even ponder such a question flatter themselves. Dr. Robert Lynn, longtime president of Louisiana College, tells a story that puts the "what is said" part very much in perspective. One day in a grocery store, he was approached by a 30-something lady who flatly said, "Dr. Lynn, you spoke at my high school graduation, and you said something that absolutely is not true!" He stopped his cart, pondered her allegation, then asked what, pray tell, HE SAID that was not true.... "You said that we wouldn't remember a thing you said at graduation, and I did," she blurted. Immediately, he thought about serious nuggets of wisdom he may have left at her program. None coming to mind, he asked, "And what do you remember?" Her quick answer: "What I remember is that you said we wouldn't remember a thing you said that night!" Well, at least she remembered his face! (One friend, in his twilight years, was disarmed by the dreaded and oft-heard challenge: "You don't remember me, do you?" Perhaps abandoning for the first time his penchant for being diplomatic, he smiled at the questioner, saying, "Lady, everything about you is familiar except your name and your face....")

◆ ◆ ◆

THERE'S NOT A LOT in the policy manuals about "how to do commencements." They are usually held in late May or early June, and, because they are big deals, they are often "standing room only" affairs, in some cases relegated to the football field. In these outdoor facilities, superintendents and their colleagues, their nerves already twisted, singed and the last ones "gotten on to," glance skyward, knowing that if there's going to be just one thunderstorm during a three-month period, odds are better than even it will occur—or threaten to occur—during this hallowed hour. In such cases, they go to Plan B, which usually means sloshing into the gymnasium or auditorium, where the sound system won't be any better, and speakers must compete even more forcefully to be heard over the sounds of crying babies, snoring grandfathers and box fans....

During our five years in Snyder, rain was a factor at just one graduation. Typically, the ceremony was held in the courtyard, where graduates (and a few others) were seated, and the masses stood. We were to have an "extra special" commencement speaker—Tarrant County Junior College Chancellor Joe B. Rushing, my old boss from Fort Worth. When the crowd had gathered—perhaps 1,500 or so people—it was apparent that a deluge was certain. What to do? Everyone wouldn't fit inside the gymnasium, and the fine arts auditorium was even smaller. I happened to spot Evelyn Davies in the audience, and recalled that she had made nice remarks at the graduation and capping ceremonies for our nursing graduates earlier in the day. Nervously, I rushed over to her, eager to know if she happened to have her morning remarks with her. "They're in the car," she answered....

I then asked candidates for the Associate in Applied Science degrees to proceed to the gymnasium, where I would present degrees before introducing their speaker,

Dr. Rushing. I asked candidates for the Associate in Arts degrees to retreat to the auditorium, where the speaker would be Evelyn Davies, who was a well-known local rancher, civic leader and friend to education; her remarks would precede my conferring their degrees. It worked! Though I didn't get to hear either speaker, I was able to confer all the degrees, we all stayed dry and Dr. Rushing was able to add to his "now I've seen it all" list. And Mrs. Davies, who at sunrise had never made a commencement address, before sundown had made two! Her topic, you ask? "Grace Under Pressure."

IN TEXAS, THERE are ten family members and friends—on the average—present for each graduate. This number varies, often depending on how aggressively graduation invitations are dispensed. Typically, graduates send invitations to family members as far removed as third cousins (and all the ones they can find addresses for with the title "great" in front of grandmother/granddad, uncle/aunt.) The motive? Oh, they can come to the ceremony if they choose (often one in a couple wouldn't miss it, and the other one is "sentenced" to attend.) Far more important, though, is the presumption that one invitation mailed amounts to one present received. (Yes, cash is acceptable....)

A neighbor, chaffing a bit that the spring of the year not only means paying income tax, but also buying a bevy of graduation presents, swears that he received one invitation addressed to "occupant." One ingenious candidate, desiring to send far more invitations than he could afford to mail, figured he was really on to something when he devised a fail-safe plan to mail more than 300 of them without spending a single penny on postage. Why, he was saving more than a hundred bucks! He shared his plan with just a few: "I have addressed all the envelopes to me," he confessed. "And I write the names of people I REALLY want to receive them in the upper left-hand corner. Then, I mail them. The postal folks, seeing no postage on the envelopes, have to return them to the sender, whose names they see in the upper left-hand corner...."

A BOOK COULD be written, no doubt, on the many pranks creative youngsters have planned and executed at graduation. Though solemnity and pomp still hold forth in a minority of cases, there seem always to be ways for the event to be remembered in a humorous way, if not a drop-dead belly laugh. For the most part, superintendents and others committed to a ceremony of dignity fail in varying degrees. In some cases, the trouble at graduation is proportionate to the number and type of threats made before the ceremony. Sometimes blank diploma covers are handed out, with the real sheepskin provided for insertion after proper behavior is evidenced. But it would take the kind of security efforts in place since 9/11 to search guests at commencement ceremonies to remove signs, cowbells and, of course, the noise-makers that have become standard fare for graduation programs far and wide—air horns. Also, there's little way to stifle leather-lunged friends or relatives who, by gum, are going to be heard!

It's fun to study expressions of graduates filing in. The pianist or organist, almost always playing "Pomp and Circumstance," usually plays very slowly, and the kids having successfully completed their courses of study march slowly to their seats, perhaps wondering why the Greeks introduced mortar boards, and why we call them that? (One contemporary says they are square because if they weren't, kids would insist on wearing them backwards....) Moms—almost never dads—worry that the graduates might not have read the instructions about what to wear—and what not. It is with good reason! If they read, they forget, and, despite senior sponsors begging them not to chew gum, for some, this request is akin to asking them not to blink. Not only do they forget to toss it, they chew it furiously, as if there's a prize for the most vigorous gum chewer.

Wary administrators watch the honorees during speeches, songs and pledges, like lookouts on ocean liners scanning for icebergs. They watch for notes being passed, whispers being shared, objects being unveiled from beneath the floor-length robes. Sometimes, the prank is nothing more than each graduate "palming" a marble into the superintendent's hand when handshakes are exchanged. For such goings-on on a football field, this is no problem. The superintendent can drop them, toss them or kick them. It doesn't matter. Folks in the stands are far enough away not to notice, and the marbles make no noise when they hit the turf. Where there is a solid floor and closer quarters, however, it is a challenge for the awarder of diplomas to be quick enough to place each marble in a pocket before the next candidate steps forward—usually about a half-dozen seconds later. When the senior classes are large, some superintendents are careful to have pant pockets altered to the extra-large size, reinforced to hold dozens of marbles….

◆ ◆ ◆

No doubt one of the smallest graduations ever occurred in 1968—at the Tarrant County Junior College South Campus. It was in its first full year of operation, and it had occurred to exactly no one that there would be any need for commencement exercises so soon. Hold on a minute. It seems that a student transferred to the campus on opening day, needing one year to complete his graduation requirements—the very ones printed in our college catalog. The student called find out when and where graduation ceremonies would be held. I told him we'd call him back.

I huddled with Dr. Rushing, and we determined that the simplest and best thing to do was turn this snafu into a "media event," so we did. The candidate sent out a few invitations, and members of his family and a group of friends gathered in the Student Center. We had soft drinks, and a tape recorder blared out music for the processional and recessional. TV news people were on hand to chronicle the event. I introduced Dr. Rushing, who made brief remarks. Then, we handed the sole graduate his diploma, he filed out, and graduation was over—no doubt, in record time. That TCJC ceremony likely received more media coverage than any in the successive years. In the meantime, many thousands have received degrees, with the county's largest auditorium packed out….

◆ ◆ ◆

SOMETIMES, MOTHER NATURE has more tricks than mere deluges. During my presidential years at Howard Payne University, I participated in some 20 graduation exercises, always handing out diplomas after spouting out the legalese about the "authority vested (or as some say, invested) in me by the blah, blah, blah."… I was still a program participant during my Chancellor years after a new president was named. At his very first graduation, Mother Nature arrived in full force. The event was at Brownwood Coliseum, and as usual, there was a capacity crowd of more than 3,000 folks. A blue curtain, perhaps 20 feet tall and 40 feet wide, hung behind the platform where dignitaries were seated. Just before the program opened with prayer, doors were opened simultaneously at both the front and rear of the coliseum. Wind rushed in from the back door, and I saw looks of sheer terror on faces in the audience as the curtain collapsed over me and the entire platform party. Thankfully, no one was hurt in the least, and I had the chance to say to my successor, Dr. Rick Gregory, "This NEVER occurred when I was president.…" (This would have been a natural for funniest videos, but somehow, it was never sent in.)

◆ ◆ ◆

IT SHOULD BE noted, too, that most graduates, most of the time, really want to do graduation right. In fact, they are so pre-occupied with doing it right they are pre-ordained to blunder it big (typically in ways that can't be anticipated)! Very often, planners identify key graduates who sit on the ends of each row. They are schooled in exactly which foot to lead with, when to go on the stage, to take diplomas in left hand to leave right hand free for handshakes, where to stand for photographs, etc. Then, others are asked to "just do what the person in front of you does." Oh, how Dr. Rodney Bowden, now a member of the faculty at Baylor University, wished he could have heeded this advice! After all, there were two doctoral candidates crossing the stage whose last names alphabetically preceded "Bowden." But, hey, he was 28 years of age, and had done this graduation degree thing twice earlier for undergraduate and masters degrees. The only substantial difference was that this time, he would be hooded.

Engaged in staring toward the audience to locate his family as his name was called, Rodney walked toward center stage, startled a bit that there was a small, box-like obstacle in his path. In a flash, he thought about Olympic winners, and how they mounted steps to receive their medals. These Aggies really knew how to show off their doctoral candidates, he thought as he mounted the box. Many of the some 14,000 people in attendance at Texas A&M University started laughing, and a member of the platform party pointed toward the box. Meanwhile, his intuitive wife, Heather, who saw it coming, was busy with her camera—she shot the scene at just the precise moment. Another platform member whispered, "Don't worry about it."

But, he was worried. It became clear to him that he needed to step down, so he did. When he did, his 6'1" frame was back in the same zip code with the guy holding the hood. He was 5'6", and it was his box. Without it, the "hooder" would have had a better chance of tossing the hood over Rodney's head lasso style. He calmly stepped up on the box, completing the hooding ceremony for Dr. Bowden....Unwittingly and unintentionally, Rodney immediately became the punch line of an Aggie joke! The crowd roared....Rodney couldn't get off the stage quickly enough, and only when he crossed in front of the stage did he see a doctoral candidate "do it right," standing obediently in front of the box. He spent the rest of the ceremony shrinking down in his chair. When he and the other graduates left the arena, he heard the giggles and felt the finger-points as he passed each section. And he still had to face his family and fight a losing battle with Heather to destroy the negative. Now, several years later, when she hears Rodney recounting his graduation faux pas at parties, she can quickly produce the tell-tale box photograph as evidence!

◆ ◆ ◆

SOMETIMES, FOLKS WHO have worn doctoral garb for many years can foul up greatly! I speak as one who has. During my presidential years, I frequently attended inaugurations of other presidents. Usually, we were advised to wear academic regalia and to sit with fellow presidents in a designated area. Sometimes, though, the procedures change. And that's what happened at the inauguration of Dr. James Hindman as president of Angelo State University in San Angelo. I scribbled the time and date of the event on my calendar, tossing the invitation aside. Academic gear in hand and just 100 miles to drive, I headed for San Angelo.

Upon arrival, I started looking for my presidential colleagues from around the state. They were nowhere to be found. As the processional began, the lady who seemed to be in charge of organizing the event said, "Just march in with the platform party." I did so, thinking I could peel off to a chair upon entering the coliseum when I spotted my colleagues. But, there was no place to peel off, and I saw no familiar presidential faces.

Up I went onto the stage, silently praying that they wouldn't be one chair short. Alas, they were! Thankfully, a university vice-president next to me urged me to relax during the singing of the National Anthem. "Semi-relaxed" was the best I could muster, because it was evident that the other two dozen or so folks on the stage—all of whom had clear reasons to be there—stood in front of chairs. I was standing in front of nothing. Just before reaching the "home of the brave," a custodian behind the stage slipped me a chair.

Thankfully, we all sat down. Then, the emcee introduced everyone on the platform, except, of course, the one mystery guest who arrived unannounced.... Following the introduction of platform personalities, he mentioned that there were numerous area presidents in the audience, and they were asked to stand. Well, I didn't stand, because I noticed they were attired in business suits. Obviously they remembered a **bold-faced** sentence on the invitation to the prexies: "**It will not be necessary to wear academic regalia...**." Upon arrival home late in the day, I wrote a red-faced letter of apology to Dr. Hindman, who sent a quick note back. He was in no way offended but did mention that "everyone wondered who the guy was without a chair when we reviewed the video!"

◆ ◆ ◆

ON ONE OCCASION, after driving some 200 miles to address about 30 graduates of a Christian high school, the setting was foreboding from the "git-go." The honorees' chairs—two rows, 15 across—were in good order, and in retrospect, nothing else much was! The event was held in a creaky old gymnasium. As the sun set on that humid June day, thermometers stood at 100+ degrees; it was stifling in the gymnasium, where huge homemade box fans were placed on each corner of the playing court. They wheezed and squeaked, doing little more than relocating hot air.

Crowds came early, and soon all the bleachers were full. (The bleachers, of course, were the kind with no back support, unless one considers the legs of folks in back such support, and some did.) A hundred or so guests stood behind the graduates, and behind them, crying babies were walked about by folks who didn't see fit to engage babysitters, or maybe couldn't find any....I remember thinking that things just couldn't get any worse, but they could!

The young principal, perhaps in charge of his first graduation exercises, seemed tense. I noticed he had a checklist, but I am pretty sure he departed from it, and, if he's still in the school business, I doubt that he will ever make such a departure again....

Things were going about as well as they could in the over-stuffed, over-heated and over-attended event. The principal had followed his checklist carefully, introducing the important school figures, presenting the valedictorian and salutatorian for their brief addresses, leading in the prayer and Pledge of Allegiance. Now it was time for the prospective graduates to receive their degrees, moving their tassels to the other side of their caps as they marched from the stage. But wait! In one single sentence—one not on the agenda, yet uttered with the sincerity given to lightning bolt pronouncements hammered out on Mount Sinai—the evening headed south—in free fall!

"If any of you parents want to come to the stage when your graduate is awarded the degree, feel free to do so, thanking any teachers you might want to acknowledge for being particularly helpful to your child." Parents' mouths dropped open. I pinched myself to make sure I wasn't dreaming. I simply could not believe what I had just heard. I prayed that the first recipient's mom or dad would NOT feel the need to accompany the graduate, because I knew that moment would set the tone for the other 29 honorees.

Maybe the air was too hot, thick and heavy for prayers to get beyond the bleachers. When the young lady's name was called, her mother was only a split second behind her, eager to grab the microphone, calling out names and pointing out teachers who had been so instrumental in her daughter's reaching this pinnacle in her life. She sobbed, dabbed her eyes and blew her nose. She thanked most of the school personnel in the audience. I timed her; more than five minutes passed before she went back to her seat, and her daughter finally got her diploma, hustling off the stage. I knew that the pace usually estimated for the awarding of degrees was 4-5 graduates per minute. Horrors! It was going to be a very long night.

As the program dragged on, all the parents didn't take five minutes—a few took several more, but most required a few less. Still, more than an hour and a half had passed since the first diploma was handed out—and I hadn't been introduced yet.

The program had begun at 7:00 p.m.; it was 9:45 p.m.—almost three hours later—when the principal introduced me with a generous and lengthy oration. I could sense pent-up groans from the several hundred persons gathered. It occurred to me that many guests had to be beyond uncomfortable. I also knew the graduates had several activities planned for the rest of the night. It was clear what I needed to do, and I was determined to do it: And that was give a KISS speech (Keep It Short, Stupid).

The only thing I had going for me was that the couple of dozen babies whose crying drowned out the speaker system during most of the evening were now slumbering on the tired shoulders of weary relatives. I thought briefly of Dr. Theodore Seuss Geisel (better known as "Dr. Seuss" to the millions of pre-schoolers who are enchanted by his many books), and how he handled a graduation speech assignment at Lake Forest College. They said he set a record for brevity. Dr. Geisel entitled his remarks, "My Uncle Terwilliger on the Art of Eating Popovers," saying:

> My uncle ordered popovers
> From the restaurant's bill of fare.
> And when they were served
> He regarded them
> With a penetrating stare...

Then he spoke great words of wisdom
As he sat there on that chair:
To eat these things said my uncle,
You must exercise great care.
You may swallow down what's solid,
BUT...you must first spit out the air!
And...as you partake of the world's bill of fare,
That's darned good advice to follow.
Do a lot of spitting out of hot air,
And be careful what you swallow.

And then, he sat down. Had I been a national personality like Dr. Geisel, perhaps I would have had such courage and judgment to try to go for his brevity record. (But, I'm not, and I don't....) But, I came close. I spoke briefly, beginning this way: "I know how difficult it is for those in the back to stand up; verily it is not much easier for you in the bleachers to sit up. I also know how late tonight the graduates will stay up, so I pray God will help me know when to shut up!"

There was immediate applause. The audience was mine after all. But I had "said my piece" within five minutes after I was introduced. (The introduction took more time than the speech.) The principal's face told me he felt he had been rescued. The recessional was quickly paced, and the program was over just as the 10 o'clock news hit television sets across the land. I suspect this principal never again involved parental participation in this way. If he did, I trust he didn't invite a speaker as well—certainly not one who traveled 200 miles to get there....

◆ ◆ ◆

Sometimes graduation speakers are "second choices," or even further down the list. I know I have been. In 1984, when I was president of Western Texas College in Snyder, a senior class president in the tiny West Texas community of Rule, an hour's drive from home, called to invite me to speak at commencement exercises the upcoming Friday night—just three days away. My calendar was clear, and sensing the plea in the young man's voice, responding affirmatively seemed a small thing to do. "Who stood you up?" I laughed, never dreaming what his answer would be.

"Sir, it was President Reagan," he blurted. "We invited him last summer, and his secretary said his itinerary wouldn't be firm for several months. We got another letter in December saying our invitation still was being considered, and then yesterday, we got a phone call from the White House saying that he couldn't come. But our class voted, and we still want "presidential remarks," so we hoped you could come...."

Wow! I had subbed for governors a few times, but never a sitting United States President! For the folks of Rule, this was a monumental step down, from the president of our 50 states to the president of one of our state's smallest community colleges! Come Friday, I was off to Rule, knowing that they wouldn't play "Hail to the Chief," but that no matter what I said, they would hear "presidential remarks," so to speak....

◆ ◆ ◆

There were hundreds of graduation speeches, but two others stand out. One was at London, Texas, and the other, at Old Glory, Texas, separated chronologically by some 35 years. In current educational vernacular, these were CTD schools. (CTD translates to "circling the drain.") The schools had a common distinctive. They both served communities dwindling in population, and they both were nearing the end.

Speaking at London was foreboding because I had never made a commencement speech before. I was a mere college senior, and don't recall how it was that I was chosen to make the talk. What I do remember is that the class was small (possibly five candidates), and that mainstays in the tiny school were the superintendent and principal. They happened to be sisters who had given most of their professional lives to that little school in the hill country, serving not only as administrators but also as teachers. The professional staff could be counted on one hand, yet there was a sense of pride and distinction that strongly supported the position that students in small schools are well-served.

The handful of high school students published a newspaper periodically. Though reproduced on a mimeograph machine, it was read throughout the community, taking many top state prizes for its lay-out, accuracy and content. (Give kids something to take pride in, and they do!) Despite engaging conversation with the school leaders, graduates and parents, there was a sense of sadness that soon, the school would be closed. And, but a year or so later, it was, and a big part of the little community died with it....

◆ ◆ ◆

A similar assignment more than three decades later was to Old Glory, a tiny community in West Texas. This time, it was made known to me when the invitation was extended that when the recessional ended on the commencement exercises in 1985, that school district would exist no more. Hard hit by changing times and a dwindling agricultural economy, the population there was falling fast. Like London, it, too, had been a respected school during its several decades of operation. Numerous newspaper reporters and TV people were present. They arrived early, pads in hand and cameras at the ready, eager to talk to the folks about what the closing of their school meant to them. The essence was a litany of what I had heard at London in 1961—when a school closes, a community loses much of its soul....

When the exercises started, I put aside what I expected to be the mundane when the valedictorian was introduced to make her remarks. She was bright, confident and added much-needed good cheer to the occasion. I saw the affirming faces of her parents, an Hispanic couple whose bright smiles reflected their joy. These parents, sharecroppers on a nearby farm, were watching their fifth and final child receive a diploma. And, she maintained a high standard reached by each of her four siblings—all were valedictorians! At once I shared their joys, contemplated their sacrifices and got an even stronger grip on a bedrock belief that education is a must for everyone, with parents playing huge roles in their children's educational pilgrimages.

Tears flowed freely throughout the evening. As I departed, common conversations among the few parents with school age children concerned transfers planned to nearby schools. I saw a lone flag, posted at the front of the schoolyard. Old Glory, the school, had served; Old Glory, the flag, yet waved....

◆ ◆ ◆

Back in the 1960's, eighth grade class members of Early Schools invited me to address them in ceremonies as they said good-bye to grade school and officially became freshmen at Early High School. Indeed I was honored to return to the campus where I had spent 12 years as a student. Alas, I entered the wrong date on my calendar; the class of some 40 students went "speechless." Humiliated, I wrote letters of apology to each class member. No, I didn't write **A** letter of apology; I decided only hand-written, individualized letters would be appropriate. It took several hours, but I felt slightly better than if I had just dashed off a form letter.

Would you believe that four years later, this same class invited me to speak at high school commencement? What a joy to contemplate such a corporate spirit of forgiveness! What an honor to be given another chance to speak! Wait a minute. Maybe these savvy seniors really didn't want a speaker, and they figured if I missed it once, I just might miss it again! No harm in trying....

◆ ◆ ◆

Finally, at a now forgotten commencement program, the emcee went on and on about the accomplishments of the valedictorian who had been outstanding not only in the classroom, but also in extra-curricular activities, at her church and throughout her community. A woman hearing the accolades turned to another seated next to her, not knowing that her next-chair neighbor was the mother of the valedictorian. "I'd give 20 years of my life to have a daughter like that," she blurted, and the other lady countered, "You didn't miss it far! The best I can tell, I gave 18 for her."

◆ ◆ ◆

LUCKILY, LIFE GIVES us many chances to keep things in perspective. Most all things "come out in the wash." Dallas' Joe Griffith, one of the nation's foremost speakers and authors, made wonderful tongue-in-cheek observations about graduation, including…

> Education is when millions of
> graduates put on heavy black robes
> to stand under a hot June sun….
> Therefore, we can assume that
> education has nothing to do with
> intelligence….

I think of the Greek Philosopher Isocrates, who, some four centuries before the birth of Christ, posed this question to himself: "Whom, then, shall I call educated?" His answer—perhaps that day, or maybe the next (it might have been the next month or next decade)—is recorded in the next paragraph of history books: "First, those who learn to manage well the circumstances they encounter day by day." (No doubt you think I have confused Isocrates with Socrates. This time, I am innocent. Socrates was born in 469 BC, and Isocrates didn't make the scene until 436 BC. Admittedly, his mom probably wanted his name to sound as much like Socrates' as possible....)

Let it be so underscored. And all that I have felt, learned, seen, heard or believed suggests that education is to learn—at whatever age—that life is about giving—being generous and forgiving in daily circumstances. When we embrace life this way, we make great strides toward understanding it and learning what education is most about.

◆ ◆ ◆

Chapter Twelve

With Liberty and Snowcones for All

When one is a concessionaire at heart (I popped a heap of corn during my high school years at the Sunset Drive-In Theatre), a curse gnaws from that point forward concerning inflated prices. Now on the other side of the counter, paying such prices for concessions seems terribly foolish.

Even in "pre-Sunset" years at ages 14 and 15, I was selling snow cones each summer for a nickel each, clearing three cents per cone. Norman Witzsche, to whom I'll always be indebted for providing my first job, furnished the machine and supplies, and we split the profit. Usually there was about $20 to split each week. I gave customers "plenty of juice"; this was a plea I heard almost every time from youngsters, most of whom could care less about how messy eating the treats might be. For the 10-cent jumbo cones I really poured it on. Often, parents—the ones whose jobs involved laundering the kids clothes—warned, "Not too much juice," despite fierce protests from the kids. Adults and kids alike called them "the best snow cones they ever lapped a lip over."

A quarter-century later, I was taken aback when purchasing three snow cones at a neighborhood stand. They were 25 and 50 cents each, with a nickel extra for each additional flavor. It seemed worse than foolish to spend more than a buck for three snow cones. I knew the approximate cost, and vowed—right then—to find a used machine for our girls and other children in the neighborhood.…Soon I found one. Supplies were bought, and neighbors, eager for their children to share in free snow cones, provided the ice, freezing it in milk jugs. Would you believe that the cost per snow cone was the same as 25 years earlier—still two cents each! Most summer afternoons after work, I'd chip up ice, then grind snow for the cones. Kids heard the noise and came running for the treats. Usually, a dozen or so kids showed up.

The machine also was popular with PTA's and other organizations for various fund-raisers; it was always available for loan. One time, it came back broken, and there were no available parts to fix it. The very same day, a woman called to see if her church could borrow the machine, and I had to break the news to her that it was broken. "No problem," she answered. "My husband is an engineer and can fix anything." He fixed it at no charge and the machine, now some 50 years old, has worked fine ever since.

◆ ◆ ◆

BROWNWOOD'S "MERRY MORTICIAN," Groner Pitts (my lifelong friend), heard about the snow cone operation I had going in south Fort Worth, and his prankish mind devised a plan to cause considerable disruption at the Newbury home. On Julie's sixth birthday—in the bicentennial year of 1976—two tons (4,000 pounds) of ice were delivered to our driveway. It was a hot July afternoon. Brenda knew I had planned to give away snow cones at Julie's party later that day, but dozens—not thousands—of them. She realized there was no way I needed two tons of ice. She protested to the driver, who assured her that he had taken the order himself, that it was indeed paid for, and, yes ma'am, the order was for two tons of ice....

Come party time, there were about 15 kids at our house, and all wanted snow cones. But so did neighborhood kids, and bunches of them. I'd never seen so many. Before dark, the number claiming free cones had reached 250, and the line of kids waiting for tasty treats seemed endless. My snow cone preparation was interrupted by a long distance phone call from Pitts, who admitted that he had sent the ice, and "put up a few signs offering free snow cones tonight" in our neighborhood.

By bedtime, I had gone through several gallons of syrup, but only a tenth of the ice, which, of course, was rapidly melting. Brenda and I were fully amused by the prank; then, we were hit simultaneously with the same thought—we were horrified about the invitation on the yard signs—the part about "free snow cones tonight." We knew that the signs were no doubt still out and that the next night would be "tonight" as far as the signs were concerned. We knew, too, that the July heat would reduce all available ice to a puddle, and that even with fullest neighborhood cooperation, there wouldn't be close to enough jugs of frozen ice to accommodate another onslaught. We dressed, then drove throughout our neighborhood—as well as through surrounding neighborhoods—collecting some 100 yard signs Pitts had hired youngsters to place in yards....

◆ ◆ ◆

DR. VEDA HODGE, longtime benefactress of Howard Payne, heard about my snow cone doings, and at homecoming one year asked me why I didn't give away popcorn as well. It was an easy answer: I didn't have a popcorn machine. "You do now," Dr. Hodge said. I knew she owned a chain of movie theatres in West Texas, but had no idea she had some extra machines. Soon, I headed west in my station wagon, knowing that the tall machine with red lights on top could barely be squeezed in, even with the back door ajar. It was a noisy trip home, and the machine's new home in our garage required a 220-outlet. It was soon installed, and when the snow cone weather ended, popcorn took over....

Soon I was taking long plastic bags of popcorn to my speeches, and in Snyder, it was a favorite treat of Western Texas College students and the whole community. But the big buzz about popcorn occurred in Brownwood, where the machine was placed on the back porch of the president's home. Howard Payne students always called it "the popcorn porch." Many nights I popped several batches of corn, turning on the balcony light in front of the house. This meant popcorn was available, and students could come and get it, going straight to the back porch to fill their own bags. In no time they learned that "when the porch light's on," there was plenty of hot popcorn ready. Students also said they could smell the corn popping, despite being a block away on campus. (Some soon learned that frequently there was popcorn available even when the light wasn't on, and they'd head for the porch to check. Years later, many graduates who got married before finishing college confessed that when money ran short, popcorn frequently was their dinner.)

Popcorn Porch

Here's where it was popped, bagged and often consumed. It's the back porch at 701 Center Avenue in Brownwood, Texas.

Hundreds of times I've told popcorn stories to audiences, usually including a reference to the night I saw about a dozen students approaching, each carrying a placard. I assumed the placards would have messages of endearment for the kids' president. But no! They read, "Forget the popcorn; lower the tuition!" (This was just a joke, but any mention of lowering tuition always hits home with many parents suffering from mal-tuition....) I became known 'round about for my popcorn, and soon had some long tubular bags printed with the words "presidential popcorn."

Upon arrival at Howard Payne, I realized that student recruitment must be an immediate priority; enrollment had fallen to around 700 students. When prospects visited the campus, I made sure they visited the popcorn porch and took home a bag or two.

◆ ◆ ◆

When it was time for the Youth Evangelism Conference in Dallas, I tried to figure out a way to give away small bags of corn from our van. I popped corn for several days, placing the small bags in large ones, stuffing the van full. There was barely enough room left for me to drive, and I even put a luggage carrier on top, and crammed it full of corn. Two battery-powered strobe lights would be hoisted on poles (blinking blue and gold school colors), so kids leaving Reunion Arena with the least bit of curiosity could visit the van for some popcorn, and, of course, a brochure about the college.

All went as planned, except I didn't notice the sign warning of low clearance at the entry to the hotel parking garage, and I forgot about the carrier on top of the van. As I entered the garage, a low overhang ripped the top off the carrier, and popcorn went flying! I salvaged the undamaged bags, and managed to have enough to distribute to the couple of hundred kids who stopped to see what the strobe lights were about. Back in the parking garage, hotel employees were busy sweeping up popcorn, or leaving it for the birds....

◆ ◆ ◆

James Dunning, an HPU student and editor of the weekly student newspaper, THE YELLOW JACKET, called one day. He wanted to do a big story tracing the history of my popcorn venture and do a photo shoot for a small picture to accompany the article. I agreed. He asked me to sit in a washtub full of popcorn for the photograph. My philosophy has always been to "look for reasons to say 'yes' whenever possible." Wearing a swimsuit and t-shirt, into the tub I went. Come Friday, when the newspaper came out, Betty Broome, Administrative Assistant to the President and one of my best friends, called me in my study to ask if I had seen the student newspaper. I had not, and was astounded to hear her description of the front page, where I expected a small photograph to accompany a larger article. Was I ever wrong! It was one big picture—slightly smaller than life-size—of me in the tub of corn. The article was on the inside pages, along with other pictures shot from different angles.

My wife, who has waged a losing battle most of the way to shore up my dignity whenever possible, picked up all the papers she could from racks around the campus. Alas, most students already had copies, and some already had taped them up on dorm room doors. It was during this episode that a nickname, "THE NEWB," emerged. I laughed about the incident in chapel, emphasizing that no matter what anyone thought about the photograph, I did have on a shirt and suit—albeit a t-shirt and swimsuit!

Dr. Bill Pinson, longtime Executive Director of the Baptist General Convention of Texas, received a copy of the newspaper. A friend from my earliest days in the presidency, Dr. Pinson never missed a chance to give me a bad time. He telephoned me, asking, "Did you know there's some guy in Texas who looks just like you who had his picture made in a tub of popcorn?"

It was, of course, a harmless prank. No one was hurt. And, my wife was swimming upstream concerning image, anyway. Oh, yes, during this escapade, students told me that "THE NEWB" was a term of endearment.

We served popcorn for many campus activities. Church youth camps were on campus all summer, and we always provided popcorn and snow cones for the participants. Thankfully, there was help from faculty and others; it was just too much for one person. Also, it was a given that there would be popcorn for all receptions at the president's home. During those years, Brenda and I hosted an average of six receptions per year, with attendance of 200-500 on each occasion. I always had a bunch of popcorn already popped, and I also got the popper going again when folks started arriving.

For prospective students—even just one—it was common to extend invitations to come by the house before they left town and pick up a big bag of popcorn. Many's the time I've given tours of the home—often unannounced to Brenda, even though she knew closets might be examined occasionally. Most of our guests had never seen a century-old, three-story home, and they didn't want to miss a thing! It was indeed a "Grand Central Station thing" at 701 Center Avenue.

One night, during a basketball game, the public address announcer read my note inviting HPU students to an impromptu popcorn and soft drink party at our home following the game. A hundred or so students dropped by, and we recognized most of their faces. Three of them, though, Brenda and I had never seen. Soon after arriving and touring the home, they returned to the foyer to ask which fraternity house this was....They couldn't believe it was the president's home. It turned out that they were students from Angelo State University, our basketball opponent that night. When they left the game for the 100-mile trip back to San Angelo, they happened to see the lights on at our house, and lines of cars on both sides of the street. They assumed it was a fraternity party suitable for crashing before returning to their campus!

The home, at the very edge of downtown Brownwood and one block from the campus, often was mistaken for other than a residence. On numerous occasions, people entered without so much as a knock, asking upon entry where they could see the body. Our response? "Probably at the funeral home across the street!"

Toward the end of my presidency, popcorn was needed for two events the same evening. We needed several bags to take to campus, where Dr. and Mrs. George Baker, whose combined faculty service to HPU totaled almost 70 years, were being honored at retirement. And, 100 or so Baptist Student Union students planned a cook-out in our back yard, so popcorn was prepared for them, too. I popped the Baker bags, then left a popper full of corn for the students, tossing in several dozen paper bags on top of the corn. It turned out that some of the unpopped kernels still were red-hot, causing the paper bags to erupt into flames. We had already left for the campus, so no one was at home as the flames melted the fiberglass case and were headed for the ceiling on the wooden porch. Thankfully, Danny Cullins, one of several siblings to attend HPU, came to the BSU get-together early. He raced to the porch with a water hose, quickly extinguishing the blaze before the house was damaged. Within a few days, the popcorn case was repaired, but I never again left paper bags on top of hot popcorn!

Giving away popcorn, hundreds of thousands of bags later, is every bit as much fun now as it was when the first bag was filled 30 years ago….And parasailing? Why it's even more fun….

◆ ◆ ◆

Inevitably, when old friends gather to talk about bygone years, the topic of embarrassing moments comes up. In my case, this subject could become a dissertation except I'm afraid the strict academicians deciding on topic validities would quickly stamp mine "invalid."

When asked, though, coming first to mind is a 1981 speaking assignment in Shreveport, Louisiana. Addressing the annual meeting of the Louisiana Library Association, I knew there would be several hundred attendees. I was engaged to speak by a talent firm in Dallas—a nice fee was assured—and I was determined to be "at my best." Upon arrival in the convention hall, I was at once surprised to see that the delegates didn't look like librarians. (What bad news it is that one of the things all of us do best is stereotype!) These folks looked like they could have been sliced from the center of any profession you'd care to name.

There were nicely dressed men and women; few of the latter had blouses buttoned against their necks. None had a bun of gray hair atop her head. I didn't see any people with pencils perched on their ears or stuck in their hair—or any with little half-glasses perched well down on their noses….

◆ ◆ ◆

But wait! There was one who could have been a stereotypical poster woman librarian of the 1930's. She was seated dead center in front of the podium. She had to be pushing 80, I thought, and a dour facial expression suggested that she might find nothing humorous about anything, particularly whatever I might have to say! (For her to have changed expressions, I think John the Baptist would have had to enter the hall two-stepping.)

Ten minutes deep into a 45-minute assignment, I could easily have panicked. Gripping a walker and struggling to her feet, the lady bellowed, "Well, I'm leaving!" She shuffled out of the hall, taking a minute or so to do so. It seemed longer, and my mind was whirling with possibilities of anything I might have said that offended her. If I offended her, had I offended others? What would the critique for the booking agency reveal? As I said, I could have panicked.

But, I trudged on. The group was gracious and responsive, offering warm applause upon conclusion.

When the session ended, I offered profuse apologies to the association president, adding that I had no idea what I

"Folks, you ought to be down here today for the dedication of the fountain at the Brownwood traffic circle. This fountain is just filled with spewers, and all the spewers are spewing different colors of water....Some of the spewers are spewing short spews and some of the spewers are spewing high spews, but they are just the prettiest spewers we've ever seen spew, and you're going to be mighty sorry if you don't come on out here to watch 'em spew!"—Eddie Farren, brother of Jimmy, a twin. These country/western musicians, along with their sister, Pat Davidson, owned and operated Brownwood Radio Station KEAN. None of them, however, had much experience describing fountains....

"I know there's no life on Mars. If there were, charges for calling there would be on Veda's phone bill."—Dr. Howard Hodge, husband of Dr. Veda Hodge, long-time Howard Payne University board member and benefactress, on the occasion of his receiving the honorary doctorate from HPU, several years after Veda had been so honored. "Now maybe the mail we get at the house won't be addressed to Dr. and Mr. Veda Hodge," he said. The Hodges, West Texas oil people who owned a chain of fine movie theatres, spent most of their lives in Midland. "When I was young, I liked to eat a fine dinner, then slip down to the Hodge Theatre for a good movie," Howard admitted. "Now, I prefer to eat a light lunch, slip into the theatre for a 'Lassie' movie matinee and lick on a Maalox snow cone."

◆ ◆ ◆

"I'M FROM NACOGDOCHES, TEXAS, the birthplace of the zip code. Nobody could spell it, so they decided to number it!"—East Texas attorney and raconteur extraordinaire Bob Murphey.

◆ ◆ ◆

"I WAS BORN at night, but not last night."—It is arguable as to who was first to utter this clever admission. One so credited this year was Texas Congressman Gene Green, who, during the Enron hearings, rolled his eyes when hearing their principals do the monkey-like "hear no evil, see no evil, speak no evil" bit. Speaking of Enron—and a congressman—this brings to the fore a question of speed. Who do you think were faster—the Houston Astros taking down Enron signs at their ball park or Californians taking out Gary Condit in the voting booths?

"HE WRAPPED HIMSELF in aluminum foil, painted the top of his head blue and came to the contest as a roll-on deodorant."—George Dolan, FORT WORTH STAR-TELEGRAM columnist and speaker, describing a bald-headed guy in the audience who had won the masquerade contest at a recent convention.

"HOWDYYYYY! I'M JUST so proud to be here."—Minnie Pearl, whose comedy enlivened homes on Saturday nights, when Nashville's Grand Ole Opry lit up radio dials across the land. She was a regular on the show for almost 30 years, and performed part of every decade for 60 years, vowing that she wanted to die wearing her hat with the $1.98 price tag on it....(Most of her shows we heard while eating frozen radio dinners....)

"I have been introduced, time and again, as one of the truly outstanding speakers in the country," Dr. Guy D. Newman, for 17 years president of Howard Payne University, demurred. "Of course, if you want to go into town...." —Audiences, within seconds, considered Dr. Newman one of them, far removed from the ivory tower....

"Don, when we retire, let's go into business together. We could open a minnow pond—all we'd have to do is be able to count to 12 and make change for a dollar."—Dr. Lanny Hall, long-time friend and Chancellor of Hardin-Simmons University.

"You need to go by the funeral home and sign the register; so and so died, and it means an awful lot to the family to know you stopped by."—My dad, T. J. Newbury, virtually every time we were together in his later years. It made me weary, sometimes, to think of yet another stop, and I often wished for him to let me be. One day, though, it occurred to me that he was exactly right—and that dads will always be dads. I never think of him now without wondering if I might ought to go by the funeral home and sign the book. It means an awful lot to the family to know you stopped by....

◆ ◆ ◆

"IT WORRIES ME that 99% of the lawyers are giving the rest of us a bad name."—An attorney friend who shall remain anonymous. Suffice it to say that he is not full of himself, and leads the laughter at the joke....

◆ ◆ ◆

"IF A BOMB went off here today, it would set education FORWARD by 100 years."—Don Newbury, addressing college and university CEO's of Texas years before he dreamed of being one!

◆ ◆ ◆

"THERE'S A LIGHT burning on the dashboard, and we can't get it turned off." That was the essence of the huffing and puffing of two of Texas' most distinguished educators—Tarrant County Junior College's Chancellor, Joe B. Rushing, and his right-hand man, C. A. Roberson, who was to hold the same post later. They had returned to the car rental office to register their complaint. The young man followed them back to the car, explaining that the light on the dashboard meant "high beam."

◆ ◆ ◆

"OH, LET'S DON'T send out any statements. The folks will pay when they can."—Forrest Kyle, publisher of the BROWN COUNTY GAZETTE for a quarter-century or so in Bangs, Texas. So far as I know, he never billed anyone for subscribing to the GAZETTE. Neither would he take cigarette or beer advertising. When he retired, a thousand people gathered for a football field buffet. The community gave him and Pauline a color TV set, and announced that Front Street—the former main street in town—would henceforth be called "Kyle Avenue."

Friends Like Few Others...
Two wonderful mentors have been Groner Pitts, left, and Forrest Kyle. Kyle, owner of the BROWN COUNTY GAZETTE, never mailed a statement to a subscriber. Pitts, an owner of a funeral home, never failed to send a statement.

I edited his little weekly paper for several summers. His emphasis: "Give 'em plenty of good news." A political heavyweight in Austin and Washington, he befriended all who came through his door. To him, a check was a promise to pay—NOT a promise that there were sufficient funds to cover it. The first week I worked for him, he owed me $40. Instead of paying, he asked if he could double up the next week, but, in the meantime, could I lend him $50? I could, and did. But, I always got my money. People were important to Forrest; money wasn't....

One day, while driving him back from Fort Worth, he asked me to stop at a department store. He figured his wife wasn't going to be too happy with his arriving back at home late at night, so he thought he'd buy her a present. He decided on a girdle. "What size?" the clerk asked. "Oh, just give me one of each," Forrest answered....

Carving out even a modest profit from the little newspaper was really an absolute nuisance. Besides not billing subscribers, he wasn't all that excited about selling ads, either. When money was short, he would have an "anniversary edition." He would call managers of Brownwood businesses who had advertised the previous Sunday in the BROWNWOOD BULLETIN, asking if he could pick up their ads for his upcoming anniversary edition—never mind that not only was it not really an anniversary, he probably didn't even know when the date really was. But, it was a nice calling card, and few objected. They knew how much he did for the community....

"WITH ALL MY FAULTS, I love you still."—Texas Governor Pat Neff, autographing his autobiography to his longtime friend, Wendell W. Mayes, Brownwood entrepreneur who owned a string of radio stations, including KBWD. Mr. Mayes was one of my employers during my student years at HPU.

"Hey, the whole time he was here, I thought he worked exclusively for us."—C. C. Woodson, publisher of the BROWNWOOD BULLETIN, during testimonies at my Brownwood going-away party held at Groner Pitts' home in 1963—just before I dragged the trailer to Alpine.... (The same night, Mayes and Kyle also spoke; at times during my undergraduate days, I had worked for all three men simultaneously.)

"You bet we've got the hat you like; you wear a size 7 1/4, don't you?"—Paul Forchheimer, who carried on the mercantile store established by his father in the 1920's. Ranchers, many of whom hadn't been in the store for years, marveled at his memory. "There was no memory involved," Paul confessed. "Except that I had to remember that three-fourths of all men wear a 7 1/4 and this helps me sell a lot of hats!"

"Is this close enough?"—Elmo Underwood always asked this as he slapped brisket or sausage up on the scales. He was the founder of the famous Underwood's Barbecue Cafeteria in Brownwood—an establishment so favored that thousands of people often drive a great many miles out of the way just to dine there. (When Mr. Underwood founded the place in the 1930's, it was little more than an enclosed barbecue pit, with a roof top and screened sides. It was then strictly a take-out business.)

Now, back to "Is this close enough?" Invariably, customers would ask for "about" so much money's worth or "about" so much weight. If they asked for "about $2 worth," Mr. Underwood usually answered that there was $2.25 on the scale.…Or, if they wanted two pounds, he might answer, "This is two pounds and five ounces." He indicated that he had sold hundreds of tons of barbecue over the years and could have guessed within a penny or an ounce each time he put meat on the scale. "Not one person in a hundred objected that I had a bit more on the scale than was ordered, so I sold many extra tons that way!" he laughed. (I remember him well. In the early 50's, my granddad Jim Gotcher worked for him, arising at about 3 a.m. each day to get the fire going in the pit. Maybe getting up so early over the years dimmed his judgment on buying me a good birthday present back when he gave me the stupid bell!)

Underwood's is now operated by second generation owner Leonard, and his two sons—Paul and Leo—who, like the founder, always have good words for folks. (Leonard, a longtime member of the Board of Trustees, and his family have been very generous to HPU.) These second and third generation Underwoods are known for carrying around hot rolls, bantering, "Hot rolls, fresh from the oven! Want some more? Need extra butter? Mighty good with honey…."

Just thinking of those Underwood's rolls and Momma Underwood's fried chicken, can lead to serious salivating, and so can the thought of my mom's biscuits….

"These biscuits are as good as I've ever eaten," said S. Truett Cathey, founder of Chick-Fil-A and a guest in our home when he visited the campus to speak in chapel. Mom was perfectly happy to fix a big breakfast, and she loved his compliment! When we left for the campus, he hugged my mom, sticking several coupons for free Chick-Fil-A sandwiches in her apron pocket.

"Why thank you kindly—you didn't need to do that," she said, "But I do have a hankerin' for those sandwiches, and I'm much obliged to you. Maybe I'll see you when I'm out at the mall—which shift do you work?" (I explained to her later, as best I could, that he owned a thousand stores, but that really didn't matter to her!)

"HIDY, NEIGHBOR! What can I get for you today?"—Red Keeler, owner of Brownwood's first Dairy Queen. That seems like such a hokey line today, but during my youth, many customers were referred to as "neighbor." Merchants today might want to consider such folksiness. Though I doubt that he was trained in the art of sales, it was clear that his care came from deep within him. He looked us straight in the eye. He congratulated us upon our order, usually saying, "Good choice. I had one of those earlier today." We kids giggled at his never measuring the milk shakes properly. "Well, I do declare, I got too much in that mixer, didn't I?" he would laugh. "Let me just pour the extra into this little cup for you to take along for later." We were—as we'd been taught to say—much obliged, thankful, yet again, that he was generous on the measurement.

Years later he, like Mr. Underwood, admitted that he knew exactly how much to put in, but why not give the folks a little extra? Makes them come back. As I think back, at most places where they got too much stuff in the mixer, the young soda jerks would pour the excess into a small glass, and start gulping it down before we went out the door. "He's drinking part of my milk shake," I remember grumbling….

"God welcomed Dr. DeWitt Reddick home from vacation, and even wanted to see his slides."—Part of the eulogy to this long-time teacher/author/friend whose name was synonymous with integrity during his more than 40-year pilgrimage at the University of Texas School of Journalism. He was Dean of the School for many years, and hundreds of educators were privileged to write their master's theses under his direction. I was one of those so honored. The day following our wedding, Brenda and I drove through Austin to turn in the finished work. He had already perused all chapters except the last one, and in it, he spotted a typographical error. I had spelled "Forrest" (as in Kyle, the publisher) with three "r's." By all rights, he could have asked me to re-type the page. "You are on your honeymoon," he said, "So let's just ink this correction in…."

"Pardon such a tardy reply. I'm further behind with my correspondence than I am with my laundry."—Erma Bombeck, syndicated columnist replying to a complimentary letter. It was typed on a continuous roll of copy paper, circa 1972, then ripped from the carriage of a standard Underwood typewriter. She scrawled "Erma" across the bottom with a copy pencil. (I just don't believe an agent would have been creative enough to "plan" such a clever response. I'll always believe it was Erma being Erma....)

"I'VE INVENTED A duck call so authentic that it attracts wooden decoys."—This claim of friend Choc Hutcheson in Lubbock won first place in the Burlington, Wisconsin, Liars' Club contest in 1961. Annually for many years, news wire services around the globe announced the winning fibs and their authors. Choc was mailed a make-shift award, but it wasn't sent to him until he had provided a letter of promise that he would return it prior to the 1962 contest. Upon receiving the award, he sent word to the Burlington club to consider his letter promising to return the award as HIS entry in the next contest!

"WHAT'S TIME TO a hog?"—An unnamed freshman at Early High School, who was seen tying ropes around the necks of his hogs, leading them—one at a time—to the watering hole. The process was taking quite a while, and it was our agriculture teacher, Mr. Wheeler, who was watching. He asked, "Couldn't a lot of time be saved if you took the water to the pen?" Then, came the answer quoted above....

"THOSE ELECTRIFIED SEATS work every time, don't they?"—Comedian Red Skelton's stock response every time he got a standing ovation, and he almost always did....

◆ ◆ ◆

"Thanks for the memories,"—Bob Hope, singing his "so longs" at the end of radio and television shows across the decades. All the verses, particularly new ones written for the holidays or special shows, were great.

◆ ◆ ◆

"I came from a broken home; most of it, I broke myself."—My brother, Dr. Fred G. Newbury, in the early grades at Early School.

◆ ◆ ◆

"There is no hope for the world outside the church and education, but it has always been that way."—Oft-stated by the venerable Congressman from the 19th District of Texas, George Mahon. This Mitchell County native served more than 50 years in public office—including Congress from 1935-1979—without ever tasting defeat.

◆ ◆ ◆

"They threw away the mold for college chancellors after creating Dr. Don Newbury. Newbury, a longtime friend, taught me many years ago never to be surprised at his antics."—Jon McConal, decorated FORT WORTH STAR-TELEGRAM columnist for some 30 years, in an account following his outing on the parasail boat….

◆ ◆ ◆

"I know about old; I remember when the Dead Sea was just sick!"—Lola Mae Daniel, Austin, Texas. As a teacher/missionary/author/counselor, this 99-year-old graduate of Howard Payne was a volunteer dorm counselor at her alma mater, starting at age 86, and continuing into her 90's. She survived open-heart surgery at age 96....

Finally, from the mouths of babes, our daughters, in their early years: At about age 4, Julie delighted in reciting the names of colleges where her mom and dad attended. She could remember Sul Ross, Howard Payne and the University of Texas, but often got hung up on North Texas State....When she just couldn't think of it, I attempted to help her fudge a bit by whispering "North" to her. "Pole!" she exclaimed. It was the same daughter who was introduced to tennis shoes not long after her first birthday. Julie became fascinated with the bow, and kept untying the strings. Finally, Brenda tied them in a double-knot; this was repeated several times a day. One day at the supermarket, Brenda glanced down at her own tennis shoes. They were tied in large, lumpy double-knots....

Jana, at age 4, had an identity crisis. "Sometimes Mom and Dad mention our two older girls, and other times our two younger girls. Why am I both?" She is, of course, our middle daughter. Another time, hearing that all the seats had been taken the night before at Arlington Stadium, she asked, "Who took them and why did they want them?"

Our youngest, Jeanie, at age 3, had trouble eating chicken salad, even when told she could eat it now or eat it later. "Well, one thing about it, it won't get any colder," she reasoned....She was in the crowd when the Dallas Hoopsters, featuring Tony Dorsett and Butch Johnson, came to Snyder to play in a benefit basketball game.

Autograph seekers followed them everywhere. Asked if anyone wanted her autograph, Jeanie replied, "I don't think I have one."

"IF THE PLAYERS today had the same school spirit ours did when I was in Howard Payne, we would never lose a game."—Tessica Martin, Director of College Information and my journalism professor for at least 10 classes. In charge of the press box at football games during my college years, she spent most of her time crocheting, glancing occasionally at the playing field, but always chiming in about school spirit in her day. (The records show that she was a student at Howard Payne from 1938 to 1942. If old brochures can be trusted, her football-playing classmates of that era failed to have the right dose of "school spirit" on a third of the Saturdays....)

"LET'S STOP AT this store to get me an apple for breakfast."—Dr. May Owen, longtime member of the TCJC Board of Trustees, spotting a supermarket at the end of the day. This distinguished pathologist—first woman president of the Texas Medical Society—frequently accompanied Brenda and me to college activities. The college's central offices in downtown Fort Worth were named in her honor. She practiced medicine for more than 60 years, never married, lived in hotels her entire adult life and never learned to drive a car. So, buying the apple on the way "home" to the hotel saved a walk the next morning. She worked daily into her 90's....

◆ ◆ ◆

"I fully believe that Heaven has a glass bottom."—Dr. Mamie McCullough, noted motivator/humorist/author and longtime member of the HPU Board of Trustees. She has made this remark to thousands of audiences across America. She also speaks of an unlikely scenario of what wealth means: "I discovered long ago that being rich meant having things in your life that made you happy—children to love, a job that made you feel useful, and screens on your windows and paint on your house." She has attained all these goals—and more—and is a wonderful friend. Mamie also is a graduate of Howard Payne, where she later received an honorary doctorate and has a building named in her honor.

"And now, Don Newbury, speaking to all good sports, reminding you that if you can't play a sport, you can be one, and a good one."—Closing line of my daily radio sports shows on Radio Station KBWD.

Chapter Fourteen

There's Good News Tonight!

During World War II, families bunched around their dinner tables as well as their radios, eager to learn the news of the day. There were few electric radios in the early 40's. Most of them were battery-powered, so adults tended to "save up" the battery for important news and/or other popular programs.

Nowadays, people my age and older keenly remember being scolded for hogging the radio, and "running down the batteries." If selfishness was involved, often it was evidenced by the man of the house—particularly if he had favorite programs planned to drain most of the battery juice. (Texas comedian Grady Nutt told about his dad's love of gospel music. When the noonday sun reached the top of the sky, Grady's dad hurried from the fields to the farmhouse where he plugged in his radio. He pre-set the dial to Dallas Radio Station WFAA, where the Stamps-Baxter quartet sang daily. This done and the volume set, he broke off the knobs, just in case someone decided to change stations. He was determined to hear gospel music immediately upon plugging in!)

Anyway, evening time was an important time of the day to hear the news, and one of the most-heard radio voices was that of Gabriel Heater, a network commentator who began each broadcast with, "Ah, my friends, there's good news tonight!" He then presented whatever good news he could find before wading into the usually grisly news from the military fronts....

We need more Gabriel Heaters. We need more people like him who help to spread an epidemic of optimism and hope, particularly in these uncertain times when even the most optimistic folks aren't really sure! It has worked historically; it can work today. Just as John Lennon claims—"Life is what happens to us while we're making other plans,"—each of us can strive to attain and to keep that onward, outward and upward spirit that our tomorrows can be better. And we must believe that we have a stake and a place in those tomorrows. Someone once mentioned that we should "live our lives in such a way that on our dying day, that's really all we need to do." What a wonderful challenge! And what a lofty goal for everyone—people of all ages....

◆ ◆ ◆

Upon leaving higher education in August of 2000, friends asked me what I planned to do in retirement. I responded whimsically, saying that when I reached retirement's shelf, I hoped to scramble down before it became dusty. I explained that I have long wanted to write and to continue a penchant for seeking the funny and profound side of daily human events. People who have meant the most to me and inspired me most have done exactly that.

I want to keep speaking to groups who want to hear me! I laughed a while back when a speaker friend breathlessly told me that he had spoken an hour and a half the previous night. "I thought the audience would never get tired of listening," he said. For me, most remarks can be completed in 30 minutes. (The straight-forward old nor'-easterner in the state of Maine made a to-the-point introduction recently: "Our speaker tonight is supposed to know a lot of stuff that we need to know. If that's right, we need to hear it, and if it's not, we need to get it over with!")

I'm not saying I know that much, but I do hope some musings, slants and stories might be worth hearing, for a few minutes, anyway. Someone once said that I could amuse myself for a full hour with a fly swatter, and it could become a half-day thing if there's a fly in the room....I'm fully aware that much humor has short shelf life, particularly when extracted from the day's news.

Take Southwest Airlines, for example. The company may well rue the day that it decided to enforce the policy of charging two tickets (on full flights) for people whose, um, foundations spread over into an adjacent seat. Thinking of this, it occurred to me that the airlines might want to "borrow" George W. Bush's acronym—POTUS—"President Of The United States." For Southwest, it could mean "Passengers Of The Utmost Size."... Oh, well, as I said, some stories have a very short shelf life....

◆ ◆ ◆

How about this one? Up front, I realize it may fall mighty close to the "shaggy dog" category, but give it a chance. Much of it is factual, and the rest, well, it could have happened!

During World War II, one James J. Kilroy became a person who inspired a myth of great proportions in the United States military. It has, in fact, defied the erosion of time. Though he was not THE ONLY—he was the FIRST—the first person to draw a cartoon of a soldier with a big nose, peering over a wall, with the words 'Kilroy Was Here' in the cartoon. It started when Kilroy, a shipyard inspector in the war, chalked the drawing and words on bulkheads to show he had inspected the riveting of newly-constructed ships. U.S. military personnel around the world 'picked up' on the graffiti, hastily looking for drawing and words wherever they went. If they couldn't find them, they made sure 'Kilroy Was Here' graffiti was in place before leaving. Thus, 'Kilroy' became the U.S. super-GI who always got there first…It was said that 'Kilroy' had been atop Mount Everest, at the Statue of Liberty, on the Arch de Triumphe and in the dust of the moon. What a timeless gem of 'gungho-ness' did this Irish-American start with this simple drawing and just three words….

Many years later, another Irish-American, Dorothy Commisky, drank from the same jug as Kilroy. She also loved her name and wanted it to become better known than his—and, for that matter, better known than any other name in the world. She yearned for her name to be on the lips of people everywhere! Fat chance. She never traveled more than a few miles from Chicago, her hometown. And wouldn't you know it? There was already a highly visible 'Commisky' in Chicago—he owned the White Sox baseball team, with a stadium, 'Commisky Park,' named for himself….And, drat it, they weren't even related, even though, he, too, was Irish-American….

Still, she persevered, 'Kilroy style,' scribbling her name, Dorothy Commisky, wherever she went, writing really small when there was just a tiny space left for graffiti. Alas, within a few years, arthritis had virtually stilled her writing hand. She knew she could write 'Dorothy Commisky' only a few more times before her fingers would be silenced….She was frantic to find an alternative, and did! An abbreviation would be wonderful, allowing her to write her name a few more times in even small spaces! Oh, you want to know the abbreviation?

.com.

The rest is history….

Don't leave! I'm winding down. If you'll stay, you won't get caught in the traffic. What traffic? In Snyder, they say traffic jams clear up with the traffic light changes….Also, you might win the door prize. (Okay, so there's no door prize. There might have been!)

This one is much shorter! A little 8-year-old girl waved her arm vigorously when her teacher asked who knew the name of the capitol of our country. She answered, "Washington, D. C., ma'am." The teacher congratulated her, then asked if she could tell her what the letters "D. C." stand for. The little girl, a bit less certain, still blurted with gusto, "Dot Com!" That's it. Don't even try to coax another .com story from me. It will do you no good!

◆ ◆ ◆

DR. KENNETH MCFARLAND, longtime school superintendent who became one of the nation's foremost platform personalities, entertained and inspired audiences of all types, usually speaking for an hour or more. When he felt attention spans shortening, he would say something like, "Now stay with me. I've begun my descent; there could be 'touch down' in just a few minutes—unless I decide to circle the airport a few times...."

◆ ◆ ◆

I INTEND TO remain the incurable optimist, admitting to being well into the autumn of my years, hoping for a long winter! (Uncle Cecil Holman always said, "Everybody wants to go to Heaven, but nobody wants to die.") In a similar vein, George Dolan wanted his pallbearers to be credit managers of Fort Worth's best department stores. "They carried me when I lived," he reasoned. "Why should they stop now?"

Optimism, to a degree, is a matter of choice. To cling to optimism is to remain goal-oriented. Who has not bought trousers an inch or two snug in the waist, buoyed by the determination to go on a diet, eat less, exercise more, etc.? Women are famous for scrunching into a shoe size a half-size or more too snug, rationalizing that their feet "were a little swollen that day," or females may flat out state that they just are NOT going to surrender to wearing a size 10 and a half! (The same goes for installment purchases; many people late in life sign 30-year home mortgages. But, let's don't get too personal....)

◆ ◆ ◆

We called Wheeler Worley "Mr. Optimist." Retiring at the traditional age after a career spanning some 35 years in the railway postal service, he wasn't even close to slowing down. This man, after spending most of his adult years sorting mail in jostling railway cars between Fort Worth and Galveston, applied for a temporary job as secretary of the Optimist Club of Fort Worth. (This was the club famous for selling thousands of Christmas trees annually, with all proceeds going to fund youth projects. Members quickly learned the key to sales meant keeping a "sold" sign on a tree at the front of the lot. Many customers, searching a half hour or more on the spacious lot and sizing up hundreds of trees, often lamented, "Gee, if I could only have that tree with the 'sold' sign on it." We had quick response: "You know, the lady who wanted that tree was to be back here an hour ago; if you want it, it's yours!" Ring up another sale, pull out another "sold" sign....)

Worley no doubt had all the stuff optimists are made of, but it became official over the better part of the NEXT THIRTY-FIVE YEARS—essentially the same span of his first job. He drove to work daily at the Optimist Club office downtown. He edited a weekly newsletter, helped to find strong weekly programs and challenged club members to "just ask" prospects. "You have to ask them," he said.

Soon his temporary job became permanent. The club, some 500 members strong, became the largest Optimist Club in the world. He was revered throughout Optimist International as "Mr. Optimist," and even in his 90's drove his car downtown to serve Fort Worth Optimists. If there happened to be an ice storm, he simply made the couch into a bed. He began his second retirement at age 93, dying five years later. Always quick with a quip, Wheeler was ready for the expected question on his 90th birthday. The newspaper reporter asked for the attribution most critical to his attaining 90 years of life. "Being born in 1895, I expect," Wheeler answered....

He promoted, believed in...yes, even daily lived, all the lines of the Optimist Creed. It officially became the organization's creed in 1922, but was originally published in Christian D. Larson's book, *Your Forces and How to Use Them*, published in 1912. Its message and popularity have been carried far beyond club meetings, into dressing rooms where coaches have relied on it to inspire players and into hospital rooms to comfort patients. It reads:

PROMISE YOURSELF—

To be so strong that nothing can disturb your peace of mind.

To talk health, happiness and prosperity to every person you meet.

To make all of your friends feel that there is something in them.

To look at the sunny side of everything and make your optimism come true.

To think only of the best, to work only for the best and to expect only the best.

To be just as enthusiastic about the success of others as you are a about your own.

To forget the mistakes of the past and press on to the greater achievements of the future.

To wear a cheerful countenance at all times and give every living creature you meet a smile.

To give so much time to the improvement of yourself that you have no time to criticize others.

To be too large for worry, too noble for anger, too strong for fear, and too happy to permit the presence of trouble.

◆ ◆ ◆

SOME PEOPLE, OF course, regard this creed as so much smaltz. It is this same group, I believe, who minimize the importance of the *Holy Bible*—the best-selling book of all time, and its "first-cousin" book in distant second place. Tens of millions of copies in all the major languages of the world have been published since the number two choice in all-time book sales was first published in 1936. It is Dale Carnegie's *How to Win Friends and Influence People.* The principles and instruction of both books, however simplistic to some, have withstood the test of time, and will remain applicable until the hands of clocks are finally stilled.

◆ ◆ ◆

THANKFULLY, *The Little Engine That Could* from childhood gets many youngsters started early on the long road to self-confidence. How wonderful that this pilgrimage is fueled by those who love us, emphasizing by word, thought and deed the principle that drives generations of freedom-loving Christian people: Every single person matters; all persons have equal worth.

It is likely that all of us have more influence than we realize and more than we deserve. At the various stages of life, it is good to reflect on those who have influenced us, and to be prayerful that our influence proves to be powerful and strong, even if only to a small group. I was exhilarated by a touching scene several years ago, soon after the Ballpark in Arlington opened. Seated in Section 221, we were waiting for the game to begin. When the National Anthem began, the audience rose; I was struck by the rapt attention of the usher, stationed just in front of our first row seats. He immediately removed his cap, placing it over his heart....

At that moment, a youngster of perhaps 10 years of age sped past, thinking no doubt of arriving at his seat in time for the first pitch. It was not to be. The long arm of the usher restrained him, and I heard the usher say, "Young man, stand here beside me and watch the flag until the anthem ends." (Yes! I thought. How delighted I was that the usher had such courage and the instinct to stop the fellow in his tracks.) But I wasn't through being thrilled....

When the anthem ended, the usher knelt and was eyeball to eyeball with the wide-eyed kid. I listened as he began a quiet explanation. "Young man, it may well be that you don't know about the National Anthem or the flag of the United States of America. If you don't, I am sorry, but it's not too late. Your parents, or preacher, or teacher or coach will tell you about them, and I hope you will find out soon what they mean. In the meantime, I know that when you hear the anthem being played, no matter where you are, you'll want to stop right there and pay tribute."

He then reached into his pocket, pulling out a dollar bill. "Take this money and buy yourself a soft drink," he said. "Oh, I know that's not enough money to buy one here, but maybe you can get one on the way home." And the kid hurried on to his seat to root for the home team….

When he left, I introduced myself to the usher, thanking him for what I had just seen and heard. "I can't be responsible for patriotism for the world, our country, the state of Texas or even the Ballpark in Arlington," he said, "But I can be responsible for patriotism in Section 221!"….

◆ ◆ ◆

WHAT A MESSAGE! Quickly to mind came those several thousand college diplomas I had signed, and the solemn charge given to graduates concerning their diplomas, with the "rights AND RESPONSIBILITIES thereunto appertaining." Further, it occurred to me that this usher intended to stay in touch, realizing that wherever he was—whatever he was doing—he could also be a positive influence—even if to just one person! Each of us should cling doggedly to some place of responsibility and influence—even if it's just one section.

Also to mind came the realization that our move from Brownwood to Fort Worth—from an environment of a college campus to a status of semi-retirement—where circles of friends and loved ones became fewer, but still precious. Thankfully, though, there can—and ought to be—even new best friends, perhaps just across the fence. While our new home was being constructed, we became friends with the Dr. Jerry Chase family; they were building their home (directly behind ours) at the same time. Quickly, we hit it off, and they even acted as though they liked my popcorn. I gave them bags regularly. I kidded Jerry, asking during our initial visit if he was "a Ph.D…or just a medical doctor?" (He is, indeed, the latter—an emergency room doctor at Harris Hospital, one of the nation's largest trauma centers.)

We decided to share the cost of a back fence. Jerry suggested we put a gate in the fence, and Brenda believes to this day that there's a good chance this was my idea. I promise—it was his. It opens from both sides. We often share food. Sugar is borrowed that isn't returned. Favors are shared, albeit some more important than others. "Would you take a quick look at this mole?" I might ask—and sometimes plead—"But Jerry, I've had this congestion for a week now. Can't I PLEASE have an antibiotic?"

Very often, at the end of his workday, we have listened to accounts of life and death scenarios he has faced multiple times in the just-completed shift. We have seen him phone the hospital after long hours on duty to check on patients. Time and again he has reiterated what parents tell their children over and over—"Be careful!" We cherish the sanctity of life, and our spirits soar that our neighbor, right over the back fence, is in the profession of saving lives every day.

At my age, it is important to freeze-frame memorable vignettes of friends and loved ones. Cherished memories already stowed away include sitting on the patio with our backyard neighbors on cool evenings. We are in awe of the stars and beautiful sunsets. We guess which clouds will first cover the moon, and into which trees a lightning bug may fly....These moments remind us of the fatherhood of God and the brotherhood of man. We are blessed and grateful that we have near neighbors whose lives are intertwined with ours—just like the good old days!

◆ ◆ ◆

We have circled, and been cleared to land; touchdown is at hand. We admit a certain sadness that the conclusion looms. For years, many friends have said, "You really ought to write a book." Now, the book has been birthed; I think I'll take a nap, and after that, I'll try to perfect the art of grandfathering....

There is no originality in my ending. I'll just duplicate what longtime amusements editor Elston Brooks wrote in his FORT WORTH STAR-TELEGRAM columns to warn of his absence during an upcoming vacation: "You'll notice I didn't say a well-deserved vacation!" He also wrote these words routinely to conclude a column: "End of the lines; everybody off." Surely I can make do with Elston's "so long", and if this won't work, I'll borrow from Looney Tunes and that giggly pig we've all heard stutter when it's time for the cartoon to end and the feature attraction to start: "Th-th-that's all, f-f-f folks!" (I'm exiting with lively music and high stepping, remembering the admonition of the man being chased out of town. He was determined to keep his head up, take high steps and make people think he was leading the parade....)

◆ ◆ ◆